SUNSET OVER CHAMBRI LAKES, EAST SEPIK

GULLIED INTERIOR OF A VOLCANO CRATER, BOUGAINVILLE ISLAND

DEW-SPANGLED SPIDER WEBS IN MIST FOREST

RAIN FALLING ON A TRIBUTARY OF THE RAMU RIVER

NEW GUINEA

THE WORLD'S WILD PLACES/TIME-LIFE BOOKS/AMSTERDAM

BY ROY D. MACKAY
AND THE EDITORS OF TIME-LIFE BOOKS

WITH PHOTOGRAPHS BY ERIC LINDGREN

THE WORLD'S WILD PLACES

European Editor: Dale Brown
Editorial Staff for *New Guinea*:
Deputy Editors: Christopher Farman, Simon Rigge
Picture Editor: Pamela Marke
Design Consultant: Louis Klein
Staff Writers:
Michael Brown, Dan Freeman, Heather Sherlock
Art Director: Graham Davis
Designer: Joyce Mason
Picture Researcher: Karin Pearce
Picture Assistants: Cathy Doxat-Pratt,
Christine Hinze
Editorial Assistant: Elizabeth Loving
Copy Staff: Julia West
Revision Staff:
Researcher: Nicola Blount
Sub-editor: Frances Dixon

Consultants
Botany: Christopher Grey-Wilson, Phyllis Edwards
Geology: Dr. Peter Stubbs
Herpetology: David Ball
Ichthyology: Alwyne Wheeler
Invertebrates: Michael Tweedie
Ornithology: Dan Freeman
Zoology: Dr. P. J. K. Burton

The captions and text of the picture essays were
written by the staff of Time-Life Books.

Valuable assistance was given in the preparation of
this volume by the following Time-Life
correspondents and representatives: Peter Allen,
Sydney; John Dunn, Melbourne; Mike Pitt, Singapore.

ISBN 7054 0165 0

TIME-LIFE is a trademark of Time Incorporated U.S.A.

Published by Time-Life Books B.V.,
5 Ottho Heldringstraat, 1066AZ Amsterdam.

The Author: Roy D. Mackay is a naturalist who has travelled over most of Papua New Guinea. He was formerly Preparator at the Australian Museum in Sydney (where he and his wife Margaret ran a weekly wildlife series on A.B.C. Television), and went to Papua New Guinea to develop the country's National Museum. After leaving the museum, he has continued to live and work in Port Moresby. He is a founder member of two scientific societies and the author of articles, scientific papers and the *Handlist of Birds of Port Moresby*.

The Special Consultants: John S. Womersley was the first forest botanist to be appointed for Papua New Guinea and has lived in Lae in the Morobe District for 20 years. He has travelled widely throughout the country on botanical expeditions and developed the Papua New Guinea National Herbarium and National Botanic Garden. He has been working recently on publications which could form the basis for a comprehensive *Flora of Papua New Guinea*.

Hobart Merritt van Deusen, who checked the mammalogy in this book, is Archbold Curator Emeritus at The American Museum of Natural History in New York City. He was the mammalogist on the fourth and sixth Archbold Expeditions to New Guinea in 1953 and 1959, and led the seventh expedition in 1964. He has written extensively about New Guinea and has played an influential role in numerous scientific societies.

Lord Cranbrook was formerly Senior Lecturer in Zoology at the University of Malaya. In 1969 he was a member of the Alpha Helix Expedition to Papua New Guinea, and in 1971 he was Deputy Leader of the Royal Society Percy Sladen Expedition to the New Hebrides.

Peter Francis is Lecturer in Earth Sciences at the Open University. He is a specialist in vulcanism and plate tectonics and the author of *Volcanoes*.

The Cover: Up in the central highlands of Papua New Guinea, early morning mist lies heavily over the grassland and mid-mountain forest of the Wahgi valley. In the distance, banks of cumulo-stratus cloud block out the high mountains and announce the approach of one of New Guinea's frequent heavy rainstorms.

Contents

New Guinea:
The Eastern Half

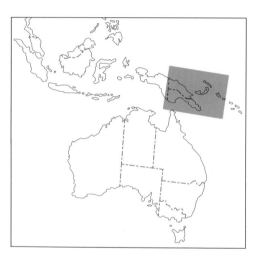

The second largest island in the world, New Guinea sprawls like a giant reptile across the top of Australia, just south of the Equator. This book deals mainly with its eastern half, the independent state of Papua New Guinea (green rectangle on the outline map above), an area that includes some 600 offshore islands. The mainland is dominated by lofty mountains, as the relief map on the right shows, and their slopes provide a series of climatic zones. Tropical rain forest is found in the lowlands up to 4,000 feet (dark green); cool mid-mountain forests grow in the zone from 4,000 to 9,000 feet (pale green); from there up to 12,000 feet is sub-alpine forest (yellow-green); beyond are the alpine grasslands and rocky summits (white). On the islands are Papua New Guinea's numerous active volcanoes (asterisks), signs of the extreme geological instability of the earth's crust in this part of the world.

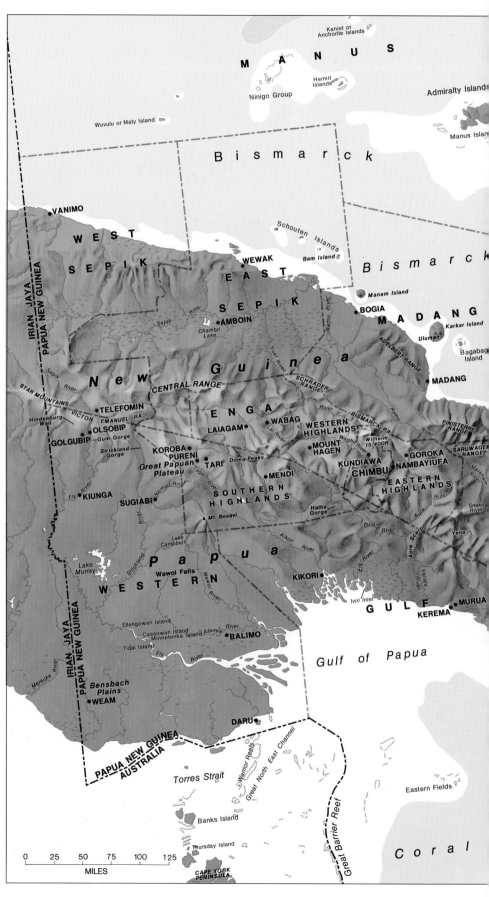

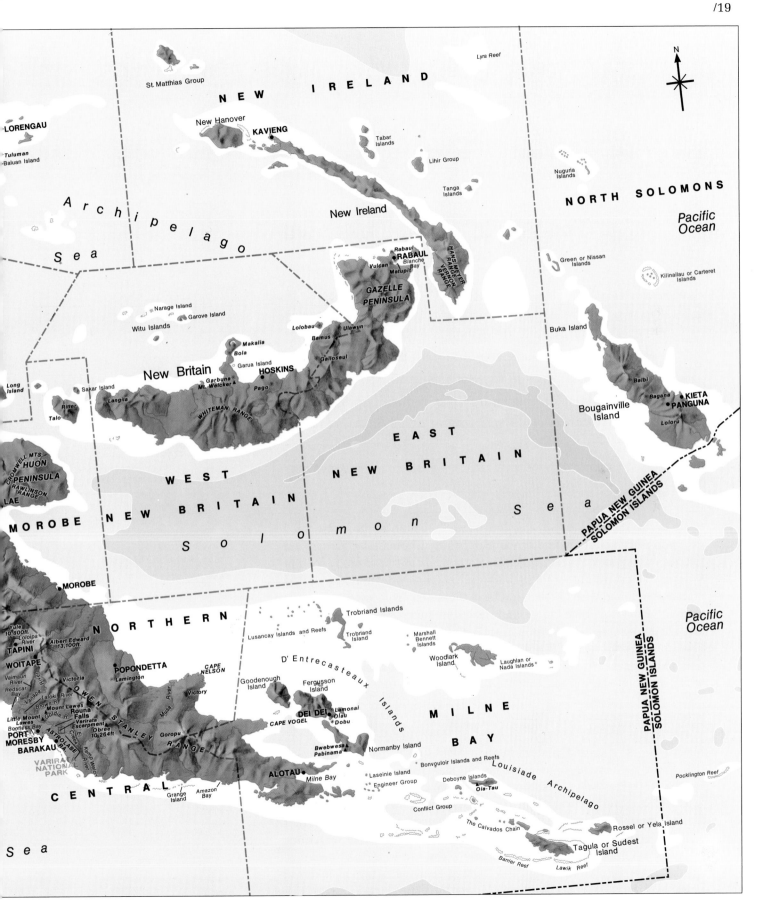

N

LORENGAU

Tuluman
-Baluan Island

St. Matthias Group

NEW IRELAND

New Hanover
KAVIENG

Lyra Reef

A r c h i p e l a g o

Sea

Tabar
Islands

Lihir Group

Tanga
Islands

New Ireland

NORTH SOLOMONS

*Pacific
Ocean*

Nuguria
Islands

Kilinailau or Carteret
Islands

Rabaul
RABAUL
*Vulcan Blanche
Bay*
Matupit

GAZELLE
PENINSULA

HANS MEYER VERNON RANGE

Green or Nissan
Islands

Narage Island
Garove Island

Witu Islands

Lolobau *Ulawun*
Bamus

Makalia
Bola
Garua Island

Galloseul

Buka Island

Long
Island

Sakar Island

New Britain
Garbuna
Mt. Welcker

HOSKINS

Pago

Bougainville
Island

Balbi

Bagena KIETA
PANGUNA

Loloru

Ritter
Talo

Langila

WHITEMAN RANGE

EAST

NEW BRITAIN

CROMWELL MTS.
HUON
PENINSULA
RAWLINSON RANGE

LAE

WEST

NEW BRITAIN

NEW BRITAIN

S o l o m o n   S e a

PAPUA NEW GUINEA
SOLOMON ISLANDS

MOROBE

S o l o m o n   Sea

MOROBE

*Yule
10,800ft*
*Lolopia
River*

TAPINI

WOITAPE

*Vaimaun
River*
*Redscar
Bay*

PORT
MORESBY
BARAKAU

VARIRATA
NATIONAL
PARK

NORTHERN

*Albert Edward
13,100ft*

Victoria
Lamington

Vanapa
Laloki River
Brown River
Mount Lawes
*Rouna
Falls*
Goldie R.
*Little Mount
Lawes*
Bootless Bay
*Varirata
Escarpment*
*Obree
10,264ft*

OWEN STANLEY RANGE

*Musa
River*

Victory

Goropu

Kemp Welch River

CENTRAL

*Grange
Island*

*Amazon
Bay*

Trobriand Islands

Lusancay Islands and Reefs

*Trobriand
Island*

D' Entrecasteaux

Goodenough
Island

*Fergusson
Island*

DEI DEI *Lamonai*
Olau
CAPE VOGEL *Dobu*

CAPE
NELSON

Bwebwesa
Pabinama

Normanby Island

ALOTAU *Milne Bay*

Marshall
Bennett
Islands

Woodlark
Island

Laughlan or
Nada Islands

Islands

MILNE

BAY

Laseinie Island
Engineer Group

Bonvouloir Islands and Reefs

Deboyne Islands

Oia-Tau

Conflict Group

The Calvados Chain

Barrier Reef

Lawik Reef

*Tagula or Sudest
Island*

Louisiade Archipelago

Pocklington Reef

Rossel or Yela Island

PAPUA NEW GUINEA
SOLOMON ISLANDS

*Pacific
Ocean*

1/ The World's Last Unknown

*When every mountain in the Alps has been scaled, and even
the Himalayas made the scene of mountaineering triumphs;
when shooting buffaloes in the Rockies is almost as common
as potting grouse on the moors . . . it comes with a sense of
relief to visit a country really new, about which little is known.*

REV. S. McFARLANE/ *AMONG THE CANNIBALS OF NEW GUINEA*

Early in the 16th Century one of Ferdinand Magellan's ships, returning
to Spain after sailing round the world, brought home as a present for
Emperor Charles V the skins of five exotic birds not previously seen in
Europe. The brilliant colours and extravagant adornments of the
plumage, coupled with the fact that from these—as from later specimens
shipped from the East—legs and feet had been removed, led to a
popular misconception that the birds never alighted on land and must
have come from some celestial paradise. In this way the birds of paradise, perhaps the most beautiful of living creatures, acquired their
name, and modern Europe came to know of New Guinea, the home of
these birds, the world's second largest island and today one of the
wildest places left on the globe.

The native people of New Guinea, some of them cannibals, wore
the brilliantly coloured plumes in their head-dresses, and the custom
took hold in Europe soon after the plumes were introduced there.
By the 19th Century tens of thousands of bird of paradise skins
were being exported every year from New Guinea. Many turned up in
the fashionable milliners' shops of Paris, Amsterdam and London, and
ornithologists were often to be found there, keeping a close watch for
the next batch of skins to arrive. Many of the rarest bird of paradise
species were named and described from specimens obtained in these
unlikely haunts. It was a long time before the collecting opportunities

improved. New Guinea was so remote, its mountains and forests so impenetrable and its people so savage that no naturalist observed a living bird of paradise on the island until 1824. Even today relatively few Europeans have watched in the wild the elaborate courtship displays for which the birds' brilliant feathers are designed.

In other respects, too, New Guinea came into contact with the modern world very recently. Virtually no Europeans settled on the island before the 1870s. No annexation by colonial powers took place until 1883, and only in the last 50 years or so has Western development made a significant impact on the wilderness.

Long before I came to New Guinea I was fascinated by the idea of reaching a place so little affected by civilization. If I could get there, I thought, I would find a virgin tropical island of rivers, rain forest and exotic wildlife. Like so many before me, I was particularly attracted by the birds of paradise. It was in Australia that I had my first impression of their brilliance and variety. After the Second World War I became Preparator at the Australian Museum in Sydney. In the museum's New Guinean section, which includes one of the best collections of native artifacts, there is a diorama of birds of paradise, displayed like jewels against a background of black velvet. No other group of birds has such a wide range of iridescent colours, decorative body plumes and crests. Some are only six inches long but the largest, such as the ribbon-tails, with their two long, black-tipped, white tail feathers, measure four feet. There are 42 species of birds of paradise. Four live in Australia (of which two are shared with New Guinea); two are Moluccan. The remaining 36 are unique to New Guinea.

As Preparator I had the opportunity to go on a great number of field trips in Australia and in due course I was asked to be the taxidermist on an expedition to New Guinea. Unfortunately I was involved in a motor accident and laid up in hospital. It was to be several years before another chance came up. This time everything went smoothly.

I was to go to Papua New Guinea. This is the eastern half of the island and includes about 600 offshore islands, of which New Britain, New Ireland and Bougainville are the largest. Papua New Guinea consists of the former British territory of Papua and the old German colony of New Guinea. Both territories were administered by Australia from the First World War onwards, and since 1975 they have been united as an independent nation with a red-plumed bird of paradise as the emblem on the flag. The western half of New Guinea, once part of the Netherlands East Indies and now incorporated in Indonesia, is known as

Irian Jaya. Its western tip is called Vogelkop (bird's head) Peninsula, in keeping with New Guinea's oft-mentioned likeness on the map to a bird of paradise. If the Vogelkop is the bird's head, the offshore islands of Papua New Guinea's coral seas are the bird's plumes.

In the first half of this century several anthropological collections had been assembled in Papua New Guinea. However, for various reasons, including war and lack of storage, they had all been shipped to Australia for safe-keeping. A few years before I arrived in Papua New Guinea, a new collection had been gathered by the then Administrator and his wife, Sir Donald and Lady Cleland, and by the Chief Justice, Sir Allan Mann. When I arrived the collection was housed in some rooms adjoining the ground floor of the House of Assembly (or Legislative Council as it was then known). The improvised gallery had only a few attendants and there was no staff to catalogue the existing collection and add to it with the aim of creating a national museum. This was to be my job, and of course my chance to see the wilds of New Guinea.

Apart from adding to the anthropology section, I began a research collection of natural history specimens, the first in Papua New Guinea. There was only one successful way to find them—to go and get them myself. I have been in Papua New Guinea for more than ten years, and during this time I have managed to reach all the provinces into which the country is divided administratively, and to visit some part of the wilderness in each. The reality of what I have found rises far beyond the wildest dreams and imaginings I had before I came here.

It never ceases to amaze me how much forest there is to explore. Everywhere seems to be covered with a blanket of various shades of green, the dominant colour being a dark green which emphasizes the extent of the rain forest. Just as the sailor sees nothing but water all around him, so it is when looking out over the mountains and plains of New Guinea: green upon green upon green of unbroken forests.

I have flown over most of this country and walked over a lot of it. Each time I fly I see parts of the landscape I would love to explore on foot, and make a mental note in case I manage to get there later. There are only two ways to travel in most parts of New Guinea: by air; or on foot patrol, as we say here, following native tracks through the jungle. Roads are scarce in most of the mountainous hinterland.

The mountains are the major physical feature of New Guinea, and I can think of only one area on the mainland where they do not dominate the view. That is the trans-Fly region of the Western Province where, it is said, there is no word for mountain in the language of the local people.

Heavy April rain drives down into the cloud-shadowed Baiyer river valley, the location of Papua New Guinea's first wildlife sanctuary.

Everywhere else along the coasts you can look up to mountains. From Port Moresby you look north to the Owen Stanley Range, topped usually by a bank of clouds. Look higher, and there, floating incredibly above the clouds, is Mount Victoria.

These mountains are part of the long chain of intertwined ranges that form the backbone of the island. This central cordillera contains the highest peaks in the Orient outside the Himalayas. A large proportion of them rise more than 10,000 feet above sea level, and many summits reach more than 13,000 feet. The highest mountains are Mount Wilhelm in Papua New Guinea, at 15,400 feet and, on the island as a whole, the Carstenz Toppen at 16,500 feet. Several of the highest mountains in Irian Jaya are snow-capped, which is surprising when you consider that the Himalayas, whose name means "abode of snow", lie more than a thousand miles north of the Equator, whereas New Guinea is less than 400 miles south of it, well inside the tropics.

The mountains vitally affect the nature and distribution of the flora and fauna, and play a key role in determining the climate. Without the mountains, New Guinea would never receive as much rain as it does—more than 60 inches a year on average. In a few places an annual rainfall of as much as 280 inches has been recorded. The island lies in the equatorial belt where the north-west monsoon blows from December to April and the south-east trade winds from May to October. As the winds are forced up over the mountains, the moisture they carry is condensed and released as rain.

Looking up at the mountains on almost any day of the year, I watch the clouds building up into great thunderheads which drop their burden of water, swelling the myriad streams and waterfalls on the slopes. After a storm I have seen small streams grow into rushing torrents, tearing at the landscape and feeding the great silt-laden rivers that pour down to the coastal plains and swamps. It is said that the Fly river, with its tributary, the Strickland, empties sufficient water into the sea to provide ten gallons every day for every person on earth.

In spite of the heavy rains, many parts of the mountains are as dry as can be. On the limestone plateaux of the south side of the central cordillera the ground is so porous that the rain soaks straight into it. I have walked in parts of the Southern Highlands and the Western Province where heavy forest indicates moisture, yet inside the forest everything underfoot is bone dry.

Other parts of the mountains trick you in this way, too. In the foothills of the Owen Stanley Range I occasionally turn off the native tracks to

The aptly named restless flycatcher returns to its nest in the New Guinea forest with an insect for the hungry fledglings. The flycatcher secures much of its food by darting after flying insects or by snapping insects off twigs and leaves. The bucket-shaped nest, secured to a Parinari tree, has been built from grass and strips of bark, and is bound together with spider webs.

climb a ridge or small mountain. The ridges are the driest places. The slopes are so steep that rain runs off quickly. Nevertheless, there is water for those who know the country's secrets. Many of the driest ridges are covered with bamboo forest, and I can walk along them for days without seeing flowing water. I quench my thirst from the small cupfuls that collect in the hollow bamboos.

New Guinea's high mountains, abundant rainfall and proximity to the Equator combine to make the island favourable to a great variety of plant and animal life. Because temperatures fall by about 3° F for each thousand feet of altitude, New Guinea has a mosaic of climates ranging from the tropical humidity of the coastal lowlands and the temperate cool of the mid-mountain zone to the alpine chill of the summits.

Each climatic zone has its own type of vegetation. Rain forest, mangrove swamps, savannah woodland, open grasslands, oak and beech forests, alpine moors—all these are found in New Guinea, and each tends to have its distinctive animal population. Human populations, too, are much divided in New Guinea. Most of the native people live by subsistence agriculture and about 40 per cent are settled in the broad, fertile valleys of the highlands. Broken mountain ranges, torrential rivers and thick forests divide the centres of population one from another, and as a result there are a thousand tribes on the island speaking about 700 distinct languages; some are pockets of people just recently emerged from the Stone Age.

The diversity of landscape and habitat is one of New Guinea's greatest attractions. While I am swimming in the warm tropical waters, among the coral reefs of the Papuan coastline, I find it an intriguing and pleasant thought that I can see the tops of the Owen Stanley Range where snow falls and ice forms. I often reflect on the description given in 1889 by the colonial administrator, Sir William McGregor, when he became the first to climb to the summit of Mount Victoria: "At night there was no trace of cloud to be seen except those that lay like lead in the great valleys below, and the stars shone out as brilliantly as on a frosty winter's night in the British Isles." McGregor examined a rock crevice one morning while he was on the summit and found six-inch icicles. A heavy frost lay on the grass. Yet here I am, within sight of that peak, enjoying the perpetual warmth of the sea.

In the course of my walks through New Guinea I often pass through a great variety of environments within a few miles. Early in the dry season, one of the most beautiful sights is found in the Astrolabe Range near Port Moresby, where the grass moves in waves like a wind-swept sea, the colour changing from bright to dull gold. Breaking out of the deep rain forests of the lower Jimi river into the swamplands of the Yuat river, driving across the great plains in the Western Province and then entering the open woodlands of paperbark or *Melaleuca* trees —such trips bring out the contrasts vividly.

Some 12,000 species of flowering plants have already been catalogued in New Guinea, but as botanists explore the more remote areas they frequently discover new ones. So 17,000 to 20,000 species would be a realistic estimate of the total number. A few elements of the flora, such as the eucalypts and the araucaria pines, are of Australian and New Zealand affinity, but the bulk is related to the flora of South-east Asia, Indonesia and the Philippines.

Like other visitors to New Guinea, I was surprised by the number and variety of rhododendrons and orchids that grow at different altitudes and in different habitats. There are more than 250 species of rhododendron and more than 2,500 species of orchid, including the giant strap-leafed *Vandopsis* with leaves three feet long and a spray of blooms extending almost ten feet. From the ground orchids of the coastal swamplands to the wide range of types festooning the branches of trees in the cool mist and rain of the mountain forests, there is an orchid for just about every niche in the environment.

Unlike the vegetation, with its South-east Asian affinities, the fauna of New Guinea is similar to that of Australia. It is remarkably rich and varied for such a small landmass, but once again the explanation lies in the multitude of habitats which the island affords. Some animals are restricted to certain altitudes or geographical regions; other animals are more wide ranging.

New Guinea has approximately 700 bird species, about the same number as Australia, which is ten times larger. Pre-eminent among them, of course, are the birds of paradise, but there are also many species of bower birds, which rival in complex behaviour patterns the intricately developed plumage of the birds of paradise. Nearly 180 mammals have been identified and described, but many are nocturnal and there may be more to discover. About one-third of the total are marsupials, evidence of New Guinea's faunal relationship with Australia. When Noah built his ark and herded in the animals by sevens or twos according to whether they were clean or unclean, he quite forgot the marsupials. His world did not include Australia, New Guinea and America, where marsupials were to be found. They are an ancient

A long-beaked echidna probes under a pile of leaves for earthworms. The echidna, an egg-laying mammal unique to New Guinea, uses its powerful foreclaws to get into the wormholes. It then draws up the worms with its long, sticky tongue extended from the end of its five-inch-long snout.

group of animals, whose young are born at a very early stage of development. After birth they crawl up through the mother's fur to suckle from a teat, protected in most cases by a pouch, until they are ready to be weaned. In New Guinea we have a wide variety of marsupial species, ranging from tree kangaroos, cuscuses and ring-tailed possums in the tree canopy to ground-dwelling wallabies, bandicoots, marsupial "cats" and pouched "mice".

There are about 130 other mammals in New Guinea, including 70 bats, 56 rodents and two monotremes—egg-laying mammals. One of these, the extraordinary long-beaked echidna, is unique to New Guinea. In the seas around New Guinea there are a dozen species of dolphins and whales as well as the quaint, inoffensive dugong, a distant relative of the South American manatee. We have a rich variety of reptiles and amphibians, and new species are being discovered frequently. More than a thousand species of fish are listed in a recently published handbook, and probably as many again remain to be described. The insects of New Guinea have been studied by the B. P. Bishop Museum in Honolulu and only one-third of the island's insect species are thought to have been listed so far. Among the insects are many magnificent moths and butterflies. The Hercules moth, which has a wing area of about 40 square inches, is the largest moth in the world. We also have several birdwing butterflies, including the brown and white female Queen Alexandra's birdwing, which is the largest butterfly known.

The profusion of New Guinea's wildlife and the possibility of discovering something new are enough to keep any naturalist occupied all his life, and there will still be plenty of work for the next generation of naturalists. I have seen a great deal myself. I have watched the courtship displays of birds of paradise. In the Southern Highlands I discovered a small, grey-green freshwater crab which turned out to be a new species. On every trip I make I find things to absorb and delight me. There is always something to see in the forests. It may be lichen on a tree trunk, the moss hanging from a branch, a beetle crawling on the ground, or simply a flower shining in the sun.

Sometimes in the forests I experience small earth tremors. In Port Moresby, where I live, few noticeable tremors are recorded, but on the north side of the mainland they are common, and in some of the offshore islands they can be felt almost any day. It gives you an uncanny feeling when, for no apparent reason, you reel about as if drunk, see trees move and the ground undulate. The leaves rustle as in a high wind and the birds stop calling. The wilderness does not seem so friendly then.

A pair of damsel flies, joined in their somewhat acrobatic act of mating, hang from a blade of grass in a New Guinea forest. Like a trapeze artist, the male clings to the grass and extends his long, thin, tubular abdomen to grasp the female round the head with pincers at the tip. Held in this position, the female reaches up to the male until the tip of her own abdomen touches the male's genital organ, just behind his thorax.

Since I came to New Guinea there have been several severe earthquakes which have demolished buildings in towns. One occurred in 1968 at Wewak, on the north coast, and another not far away at Madang in 1970. Two struck the island of New Britain in 1967 and 1968.

When severe earthquakes occur in the wilderness, large areas of forest are destroyed and may take a hundred years to regenerate. Luckily I have never been caught in a serious earthquake, but a surveyor I was talking to recently did experience quite a strong one when he was in a remote part of the country.

He was marking out survey points on mountain tops near the headwaters of the Purari river, and had camped overnight after finishing his work. Early the next morning he was sitting on one of the mountain tops with his instruments, waiting for a helicopter to pick him up. From his vantage point he looked down into a broad valley and across to the steep slope opposite. It was a calm morning with no breeze, and he thought it most unusual when he saw the trees on the opposite slope swaying in a long line as if a strong wind was passing over them. The line of motion swept like a big wave down the slope, across the valley floor and up towards him. As it reached the place where he was sitting, the ground shook violently and the near-by trees swayed in unison; then the earth tremor passed on. He said it was a most unnerving experience.

The frequent earthquakes are signs of the geological instability of this part of the earth's crust. Indeed, New Guinea lies in one of the most unstable zones in the world, and 5 to 10 per cent of all earthquakes occur here. Further evidence of the geological upheaval taking place is provided by the active volcanoes, whose locations closely follow the pattern of recorded earthquakes. There are a few vents on the north side of the mainland, near Popondetta in the Northern Province and in the eastern reaches of the central cordillera. Nearly all the volcanoes, however, are located offshore in two great arcs, one starting close to the north coast and curving up through New Britain, the other starting in Bougainville and continuing south through the Solomon Islands.

I have not seen a full-blown eruption of a volcano. I would like to—from a safe distance. However, I have flown over several of Papua New Guinea's active volcanoes and seen one minor eruption. The flight from Wewak to Madang, which I often make in the course of my work, takes me past the island volcano of Manam. The fumes rising from its peak are a constant reminder that it is potentially dangerous. When severe eruptions occurred in 1957 and 1958, the villagers living at the foot of the cone had to be evacuated to the mainland, returning afterwards to find their gardens enriched by a fresh layer of volcanic dust.

When I made one of my flights past Manam, the volcano was actually erupting. The activity, although not dangerous to the people on the island, was nevertheless spectacular. Huge black clouds of ash and gas were belching from the eastern side of the island's peak. A strong breeze blew the smoke to the west and I caught sight of the vent itself. Rocks and ash were being thrown out over the edge, landing in the litter of volcanic debris on the bare upper slopes. As we came closer I was able to make out furrows running down the tree-covered lower slopes, marking the course of old lava flows. Then the volcano was obscured by a layer of dense cloud.

I was glad to have seen this eruption, not just for the spectacle itself but because I was watching one small step in the long process that has made New Guinea so mountainous. The eruption of volcanoes, the tremor of numerous earthquakes, the creation of mountains—all these earth-changing events are part of a single geological process and can be explained by the theory of plate tectonics. The theory, still not accepted by a few scientists, is as big a revolution in geology as the theory of evolution was a century ago in biology. Its fascination is that it explains with forceful simplicity how the earth's crust evolves.

The earth is not static. It is constantly changing beneath our feet, and New Guinea in a few tens of million years' time will certainly look quite different, just as a few tens of million years ago it was still without large mountain ranges.

According to the plate tectonic theory, the outer layer of the earth is divided into huge segments or plates. The plates carry ocean basins, islands and continents on their backs like passengers, and are in constant motion. For example, the Indian–Australian plate, which carries the entire continent of Australia and the southern part of New Guinea, moves a couple of inches to the north every year. The plates move outward from submarine mountain ranges in mid-ocean where new oceanic crust is continually being created. Beneath each of these great, submerged ridges, such as the Antarctic Ridge or the East Pacific Rise, huge masses of semi-fluid rock are driven upwards by convection currents within the earth's hot mantle. Some of the rock melts to magma and is forced up and up until it bursts through the sea floor as a volcanic eruption.

The effect of continual volcanic activity along a mid-oceanic ridge is to add primitive basaltic magma, the stuff of which ocean floors are made, to the oceanic crust along the line of the ridges. The sections of sea floor, or oceanic plates, on either side of the ridges move away in opposite directions as this new material is attached to their trailing edges. Were it not for some compensating mechanism at their margins, all the world's oceans—and the earth itself—would get larger each year.

Of course this does not happen. What does happen, though, is quite dramatic. Around the edges of the oceans, the outward moving oceanic plates come into collision with continent-carrying plates, which may well be in motion themselves. Unable to continue on their course, the oceanic plates are thrust steeply down beneath the opposing continental plates, and "subducted" back into the earth's mantle. The sites of these behemoth collisions are known as destructive plate margins, for it is here that ocean crust, originally created in mid-ocean, is consumed.

The process is accompanied by great geological upheavals. Immense friction is generated between the two plates as they grind against each other, and the pent-up energy is released in the form of powerful earthquakes. As the oceanic plate plunges deeper, it gets hotter and hotter until, at depths of more than 50 miles, it begins to soften and partially melt. New magma is formed, and some of it rises to the surface, bursting through in the form of volcanic eruptions. At the same time, the overriding continental plate buckles and folds under the strain, and new mountain ranges are born.

New Guinea and its attendant islands are undergoing precisely these cataclysmic changes, for they lie directly over a series of destructive plate margins, past and present. They constitute an important part of that great, circum-Pacific girdle of seismic and volcanic activity known as the "ring of fire". Just north of New Guinea, the earth's crust is greatly tortured. It is being broken up and shuffled around in an amazingly complex fashion as several gargantuan crustal chunks grind together, now diving down one under the other, now flipping up, always battling like fleets of opposing icebergs. As the Indian–Australian plate moves steadily northwards, four, possibly five Pacific plates are coming south and west to meet it. New Guinea lies at the point of impact.

Hundreds of millions of years ago the picture was utterly different. The southern part of New Guinea formed one edge of the Indian–Australian plate; it was the continental shelf along Australia's northern boundary. There were no mountains. Sometimes the surface of palaeo-New Guinea was exposed as low-lying plains, sometimes submerged beneath the shallow waters of the continental shelf. Beyond lay the broad, open ocean. For millions of years all was tranquil. Then, far to the north, one section of oceanic crust was forced down beneath another, and the resulting volcanic activity threw up an arc of islands in mid-ocean. These islands, strung out in a great curve, were the ancestors of the present New Britain arc. In time, Australia and palaeo-New Guinea drifted steadily northwards in the direction of the new island arc, which may have been stationary or perhaps was drifting southwards.

During the Miocene, between 11 and 25 million years ago, there was a giant collision. The more westerly islands in the arc were plastered on to the north-east coast of palaeo-New Guinea. Great mountains were thrown up and modern New Guinea was created. The eastern end of the island arc did not collide, and can still be seen. It consists of New Britain, New Ireland and the associated smaller islands.

New Guinea's drift northwards as part of the Indian–Australian plate not only shows how the mountains were created; it explains some puzzles about the island's flora and fauna. Why does the flora bear many resemblances to that of South-east Asia, whereas the fauna with its high proportion of marsupials is similar to that of Australia? And how is it that outside the Australia-New Guinea region, marsupials are found only in the Americas?

Marsupials appear to have originated in North America and South America, where the oldest marsupial fossils have been found. At that time, during the late Cretaceous and Eocene periods between 40 million and 100 million years ago, South America, Africa, India, Antarctica and Australia-New Guinea were united in a single southern continent: Gondwanaland. Consequently the early marsupials were able to find their way overland from South America to Australia-New Guinea. Then Gondwanaland broke up under the strain of plate tectonic changes, and the continents drifted apart towards their present positions.

Placental mammals were able to reach the Americas across the Bering land bridge from Asia, and there they have replaced much of the older marsupial population. But Australia-New Guinea was entirely isolated from Asia, and here marsupials continued to flourish. Eventually, however, as New Guinea drifted northwards, it came close enough to South-east Asia for the flora of the Oriental region to colonize its tropical shores.

Plants can migrate over greater expanses of sea than animals. Once the distance had been sufficiently reduced, the seeds of plants common in South-east Asia were able to make the crossing to New Guinea, carried on the wind, on floating vegetation, or in the plumage of birds. Many birds, as well as insects and bats, would have experienced little

SEPIK RIVER BLUE ORCHID

An Orchid Paradise

Orchids form probably the largest family of flowering plants in New Guinea and an enchanting variety of more than 2,500 species exists, the habitats ranging from the lowlands up to 10,000 feet.

The largest blooms belong to the sun-seeking epiphytes, which live on the trunks and branches of forest trees between sea level and an altitude of 3,000 feet. Among these is the oddly named Sepik river blue orchid (left), whose red flowering spikes reach a length of 24 inches.

Although the flowers of orchids above 6,000 feet are often more brilliantly coloured than those of species at lower altitudes, the plants tend to be smaller and tougher in texture, like the cherry orchid with its mass of miniature blooms (right).

CHERRY ORCHID

difficulty in flying over the intervening stretches of sea, if necessary by "island hopping". Certain reptiles and rodents probably also made the journey from Asia to New Guinea on floating vegetation, but this was impossible for the large Asian mammals such as apes, monkeys, elephants, rhinoceroses and tigers: hence the absence of such creatures in New Guinea. Other animals such as pigs, goats, deer and poultry arrived much later, introduced by man.

Two late-19th Century naturalists, Alfred Russel Wallace and Max Weber, drew imaginary lines from north to south, separating the Oriental from the Australasian region. The Weber line, cutting through the Indonesian islands east of Sulawesi and Timor, is in my opinion the more realistic, taking into account a transitional zone that contains Asiatic animals such as tarsiers and jungle fowl as well as Australasian cuscuses and cockatoos. To the east and west of this intermediate zone, the pattern of fauna remains distinctly contrasted. But who knows? One day it may no longer be so. The pace of geological change in the New Guinea region is very fast, and the impact of man on flora and fauna is likely to become increasingly significant.

Geological changes are usually so slow as to be imperceptible, but sensitive instrument readings tell us that the island of New Guinea is moving steadily northwards. Moreover, some changes on the island can be witnessed in the course of a single lifetime. This was brought home to me when I visited some coastal villages of southern Papua where the shoreline is moving out to sea. I was chatting to an old man from the village of Vailala at the mouth of the silty Vailala river. The original home of these tribesmen was another village called Popo, now abandoned. The old man told me that the site of Popo can still be seen; but whereas, when it was occupied, the village was on the coast, it now lies in the bush about five miles inland. Over the years the river has built up the land, eroding the youthful mountains of the interior and carrying them, particle by particle, down to the sea. Obviously the process is continuing fast. The local pastor who was listening to our conversation confirmed the old man's account and proved to me that during the 20 years he had been in the village, the sea had receded some 50 yards. He showed me the original coastline near his house, and I measured the wide expanse of beach front that had been added in that time.

I feel sure that the early naturalists and explorers who first opened up New Guinea to the knowledge of the West had little idea that they were starting a new era of change, not only in the people but in the landscape itself. It is man who has brought the most drastic changes to New Guinea in recent years, and although these changes are small in comparison with the overall size of the wilderness, they are continuing. The early naturalists, explorers and administration patrol officers produced the findings from which have come the exploitation of the land, forests, water resources and mineral wealth.

One of the most active and famous—or notorious—of the naturalists was the Italian, Luigi D'Albertis, whose exploits in the 1880s earned him a reputation both for expert collecting and a complete disregard of native rights. D'Albertis was constantly on the lookout for new plant and animal species, and sometimes plundered the villages for specimens. At least four bird species in Papua New Guinea are named after him, and several others were named by him. Another naturalist of the late 19th Century was A. S. Meek, who came to Papua New Guinea to make collections for Lord Rothschild's Tring Museum in England. In his book *A Naturalist in Cannibal Land* he made comments about the country and its wilderness. He was not deterred by the ruggedness of the country which, he remarked, "seemed to be built on the 'switchback' principle. One fold of hills was followed by another." The patrol officer Jack Hides explored the Strickland river and its tributaries in 1937 and described the trip vividly. "I looked around at the dripping, moss-covered forest, at the jagged rocks of black and white limestone," he wrote, "and I realized that we could rely only upon ourselves in this place so far removed from the outside world where a cry is only to the wilderness." The area of the Strickland river is still a wilderness, and provided no oil or minerals are discovered there, it is likely to remain so.

D'Albertis, Meek, Hides and others were attracted by the wild nature of New Guinea. They had a deep love for the land and its natural wealth of plants and animals. Today they would still find a wilderness to explore and wonder at. I hope to show how I too have been enthralled by this, one of the last truly wild places.

The Silent Killers

The rain forest of New Guinea, with its luxuriant tree canopy and leaf-littered floor, provides a haven for spiders. In this dank and darkened world they find abundant supplies of food in the form of insects—and one another. But the spiders are also preyed on by many birds and reptiles, and so have developed a remarkable variety of skills enabling them to kill without being killed.

Although much research remains to be done, there are believed to be some 3,000 species of New Guinea spiders, and these can be divided into two groups according to the method they use for catching prey.

The first—and most intriguing—group comprises species that do not use webs to capture their prey, contrary to most people's idea of spiders. Some of them, like the flower-spider (right), are sedentary, relying on camouflage to avoid detection. They wait for their victims to come to them, launching a sudden attack when an insect settles near by. Others, including the large, crab-like sparassids, remain camouflaged and inactive during the day, but start searching for prey as soon as darkness falls.

The small, brightly coloured salticids, or jumping spiders, which form the largest New Guinea spider family, hunt by day. Possessing the keenest vision of all spiders, they often jump distances many times their own length to catch prey.

Even the second group, which traps its victims with webs, comprises a rare and fascinating array of spiders. Their silken snares range from simple webs of criss-crossed strands to the elaborately interwoven and symmetrically structured webs spun by the orb-weavers.

One of the most spectacular snares is that of *Nephila maculata*, a large, spindly-legged spider that produces a coarse web of enormous strength measuring three feet or more in diameter. Unlike other orb-weavers, *Nephila maculata* does not renew its web at frequent intervals but uses the same web for long periods by repairing damaged parts.

Some New Guinea spiders band together in colonies to spin vast communal webs. Suspended across forest clearings, these webs often span 30 feet. But perhaps the most unlikely, though effective, snare is produced by the bolas, or angler spider. It suspends a sticky globule at the end of a thread which it then whirls around in the air, until it snags a flying insect.

A flower spider seizes a moth that has landed on a D'Albertis orchid in search of pollen. The spider's smooth off-white body closely matches the texture and colour of the orchid's petals, allowing the spider to lurk undetected within the flower. Although its eyesight is poor, it is alerted to the arrival of prey by the slight quivering of the flower.

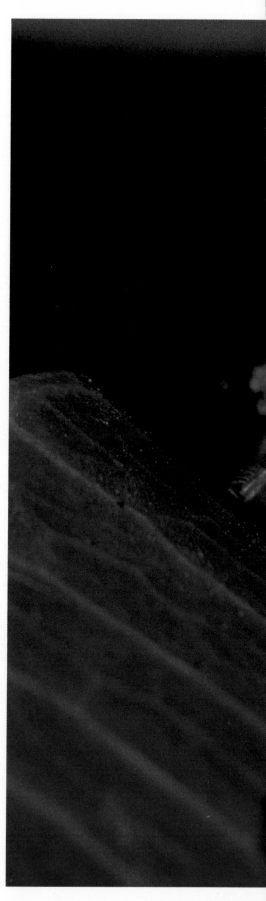

The glossy male jumping spider (above) is almost at the end of its two-year lifespan and is now ready to mate. To attract and retain the female's attention during the elaborate courtship dance, male salticids moult to reveal brilliant colours. Other salticids are clothed with iridescent scales and ornate hair tufts.

The eight sharp eyes of the female jumping spider (right), mounted round the patterned turret on its carapace or head, provide all-round vision and enable it to recognize predators or prey 12 inches away. A stealthy hunter, the spider leaps on its victim, killing it with a swift and venomous bite.

A female lichen spider (left) confuses its enemies by blending with the mottled bark of a tree, waiting for darkness to fall before starting its own search for prey. Considered to be a rare member of the sparassid family, the lichen spider is able to match various different surroundings by changing its colour.

Stretched out along a tree branch, another lichen spider (right) takes on different camouflage for a different background. It has unusual fringes round its delicate legs, reminiscent of those found in some salticid spiders. But it lacks the keen vision and jumping power of the salticids.

From its perch on a twig, a bolas or angler spider dangles its snare—a single thread tipped with a sticky globule. The angler has lost its ability to weave a web; instead it whirls the thread around above its head until it catches a flying insect which it then trusses up and devours.

A young orb-weaving spider rests on the ornate hub of its web. The doily-patterned platform spun with thick, non-sticky silk makes the spider itself less conspicuous as it lies in wait for insects. The orb-weaver possesses poor vision, but finds its prey by following the vibrations in the web.

The St. Andrew's Cross, or X-ray spider, takes its name from the diagonally crossed ribbons of silk with which it decorates its web.

A female Nephila maculata, or golden orb-weaver, clings to the underside of a twig (left), in the fork of which can be seen part of its web. The orb-weaver's spectacular golden web (above) may measure three feet across, with 20-foot guy-lines suspended between trees. The web is strong enough to ensnare small birds, and has even been used by local people in making bags and fish nets.

*Waiting on their vast, flossy-looking
communal web, hundreds of Cyrtophora
spiders appear to hang in mid-air. Their
web, suspended 50 feet above the slopes
of Mount Kaindi in eastern Papua New
Guinea, is actually a patchwork of
hundreds of tiny orbs spun by
individual members of the colony.*

A young sapling yields to the tension
exerted by a massive Cyrtophora web,
stretched high above a clearing as a
trap for the insects that flit through the
forest canopy. When a sizeable insect is
caught, spiders converge from all
directions to secure the creature, and
then begin a communal feast.

A spiny-backed spider, its armoured abdomen dazzlingly white in the photographer's flash, pulls together strands of web as it sucks the juices of a fly it has trapped. The spiny-backed spider relies on a brilliant body pattern and its three curved abdominal spines to startle and deter its enemies.

2/ Land Behind the Clouds

*The last 2,000 feet seemed to have no connection
with New Guinea, but rather to be floating in a
sea of white cloud like some ghostly island.*

GAVIN SOUTER/ *NEW GUINEA: THE LAST UNKNOWN*

Pilots of small aircraft in New Guinea avoid flying into clouds: too many
of them conceal 12,000-foot mountains. In the small museum at Port
Moresby there is a grim reminder of this danger. It is a diary written on
the door of an aircraft which flew into thick cloud and crashed on Mount
Obree, about 50 miles from Port Moresby, during the Second World War.
Miraculously, 17 men survived the crash, but only three or four managed
to struggle down through the forest to civilization. The rest died of
exposure or starvation before the rescue party could reach them,
leaving a record of their last days scrawled on the door.

It is amazing how quickly clouds can build up in these mountains.
Recently I went on a short flight across the Owen Stanley Range from
Port Moresby in the south to Popondetta in the north. I was with two
friends who had to repair a truck that had broken down in Popondetta.
I went along for the ride, hoping to take some photographs of the
mountains. We left shortly after dawn, expecting to be back later the
same morning. It was a fine day, without a cloud in the sky; but there
was a blue haze in the air, so my photographs were not of the best. The
sky was still clear when we landed. My friends were not long fixing the
truck and we were back at the airstrip at about 10 a.m. By then a thick
dark blanket of clouds had blotted out the mountain spine in both
directions for as far as we could see. We took off, thinking we might be
able to slip through the cloud cover along an 8,000-foot pass; but as we

approached the mountains we could see great banks of cloud already plunging into the valleys and obscuring our path, so we were forced to turn back and stay overnight at Popondetta. Very early next morning we managed to get through the pass before the clouds built up again. But we were only just in time: as we dropped down towards Port Moresby I turned to look back at the pass. It had already vanished.

Such incidents are common, but I would never miss the chance of a flight over the mountain ranges. On one memorable trip across the Star Mountains, near the border with Irian Jaya, I was able to look along the length of Papua New Guinea's central cordillera. The mountain tops differed widely: some were forested to the summits, some had bare, jagged peaks and others had rounded domes covered with alpine grassland. On the opposite side of the aircraft I could see the snow-capped peaks of Puncak Mandala in Irian Jaya.

From the air you can really begin to appreciate how this country's mountain backbone was formed. When millions of years ago the mainland of palaeo-New Guinea drifted northwards and crumpled into the island arc which stood in its way, great blocks of the earth's crust were thrust up vertically several miles. The tangle of steep, knife-edged ridges and deep, winding valleys are a sure sign of geological youthfulness; in fact, the central mountains of New Guinea were formed as recently as any in the world.

In the north-east, the broad, flat valleys of the Ramu and Markham rivers separate the central cordillera from the outlying mountains that run along the coast, the Adelbert Range and the four ranges which extend eastwards to the Huon Peninsula—Finisterre, Saruwaged, Cromwell and Rawlinson. From the ground, these valleys are unspectacular, but if you fly over them you can see how long and straight they are—evidence that this divide is a huge fault zone and the site of the collision with the island arc.

When you see the height and ruggedness of the New Guinea mountains it is hard to imagine that many of the rocks of which they are built once formed the sea floor. Yet for anyone willing to look, the proof is there. In the Southern Highlands, where high parallel ridges separate broad, fertile valleys, I have made many surprising finds. It is difficult country to explore because the ridges are well forested and steep. Crossing from one valley to the next by mountain trail is a formidable task, since the intervening ridge may be 800 or 900 feet high. In some places the trail is glistening wet, smooth and very slippery. In others the surface is so jagged that rubber boots are torn to shreds and even

stout leather boots can be ruined in a two-day hike. But the rewards can be worth the effort. I have turned up fossilized corals and even some whorled ammonite shells four inches across. These were the relics of creatures that lived in a Mesozoic sea at least a hundred million years ago and are now extinct. On a trail near Koroba I was examining some rocky deposits where the track cut through a little knoll; there I found the serrated bony scales of a large fossilized crocodile. It was strange to think that this creature, once the inhabitant of an ancient river estuary, had ended up petrified high in the mountains.

The central cordillera consists chiefly of sedimentary rocks derived from river silt as well as volcanic and intrusive rocks. But in south-east Papua New Guinea, along the northern slopes of the Owen Stanley Range, there is a 150-mile belt of rocks rarely found on land. These are great masses of peridotites, gabbros and serpentinites, igneous and metamorphic rocks that once formed part of the deep ocean crust, lying as much as six miles beneath the sea floor with its surface covering of sediment. Normally an ocean plate, when it meets an opposing continental plate, is forced down into the earth's mantle, never to be seen again. But in this case, when New Guinea collided with the island arc, some ocean crust rode up on to dry land and was marooned on top of the sedimentary rocks of the Owen Stanleys.

The geological upheavals that created New Guinea's mountains have left their mark clearly on the living flora and fauna. The jumble of mountains and valleys has divided the country into separate regions isolated from one another. For example, the low-lying land of the Ramu-Markham fault zone, which cuts off the Adelbert Range and the Huon Peninsula from the central cordillera, has allowed the evolution of distinct species of plants, birds and other animals.

Perhaps the most striking example of these isolated species is Beck's bowerbird which is endemic to the forests of the Adelbert Range. It is a magnificent black bird with bright yellow wing patches and a crown and mane of golden orange. There are only about half a dozen specimens in museum collections and I know of only one European who has seen the bird in recent years. It is so rare that its bower has never been described.

In the four interlocked ranges of the Huon Peninsula, perhaps the steepest and wildest mountain country in Papua New Guinea, there are are at least three unique birds of paradise. One is Wahnes's six-wired parotia, so named because of three long wire-like plumes, with oval-shaped, flat feather tips, growing from above each of its ears. It is a spectacular bird—velvet black except for a breast shield of metallic

Shrubs, mosses and tussocks of grass form the alpine grasslands at about 9,000 feet above sea level in the Dayman Range of eastern Papua.

feathers which reflect rainbow colours, a tuft of gold-tipped feathers on its forehead and a patch of iridescent blue on its nape. The parotia displays on the ground, dipping its head on to its chest and shaking its wire plumes about so much that it is a wonder they are not broken.

Among the mammals which are indigenous to the region, Matschie's tree kangaroo, a big, brick-red animal with a very long tail, is found only in the mid-mountain forest of the Huon. Unlikely as it seems for a kangaroo to hop through the treetops, this species finds it easy. In fact, I have seen a tree kangaroo leap at least ten feet between branches. Its tail swings round and acts as a counter-weight to balance the animal when it lands. The tree kangaroo is largely nocturnal and surprisingly quiet as it moves about among the branches, feeding on fruit, leaves, insects and sometimes small birds. One night in the forest, I detected the presence of tree kangaroos only when I was struck by some half-eaten fruit that fell out of the trees. At first I thought that some cuscuses were feeding above me. But when I shone a strong torch up into the high foliage I saw two tree kangaroos sitting on a thick branch, chewing away at the fruit. You find them now only in the deepest forest, because they are hunted by the local people and so tend to keep away from the villages.

Several other species are unique to the islands off the New Guinea coast, many of which have high mountains covered with dense, virtually undisturbed rain forest. Goldie's bird of paradise, for example, lives only in the rain forest of Fergusson and Normanby Islands. It has been seen by few Europeans. Fergusson and Normanby are actually great mountain peaks poking out of the sea, part of a group known as the D'Entrecasteaux Islands. On the slopes of a high, thickly forested mountain on one of the D'Entrecasteaux Islands, an interesting variant of slipper orchid, *Paphiopedilum sp.*, was discovered by an American expedition in 1956. I went out to these islands recently with a party of botanists to collect some specimens. Because of the wet weather, we decided that it would take at least four days to get there and back, allowing sufficient time to set up rain-proof camps and hunt for the orchid. But by an extraordinary piece of luck, we found it almost before we had started looking.

The day before the projected climb, three of us, with a few native guides, went up a near-by, lower mountain. We were about to start our return through a patch of secondary forest with lots of shrubby under-growth, thorny vines and clumps of thin bamboo when a German orchid specialist, who had been trailing somewhat behind, shouted excitedly for us to wait. He had found a slipper orchid—and the rest of us had

Pale blue and iridescent, a banded weevil projects its jointed antennae. The banded weevil has good eyesight; its antennae are used for olfactory sensing and perhaps also for communication. Its body coloration comes from hundreds of tiny scales; when they are rubbed off, the weevil looks black.

walked over it. After searching the area we found that they were all around us. In fact, we counted 89 specimens in an area 60 feet square. Unfortunately they were not in flower—but at least that gave us an excuse for missing them the first time.

The plants and animals of the mountains are divided not only by their geographical isolation. There is another limitation that affects every living thing along the central cordillera, the outlying ranges and the offshore mountain peaks. It is altitude. As you climb higher up the mountains, the forest changes in character from luxuriant tropical rain forest at the base to alpine grassland at the highest peaks.

I was strongly impressed by this one day while I was exploring the southern slopes of the Owen Stanley Range. I had flown into Tapini, a small town with an airstrip at 3,000 feet, half-way up the steep sides of the Loloipa river valley. Much of the hillside around the town is covered with rank grass, because the original forest has been cut down and burned to make way for gardens. (The soil will support subsistence crops only for a couple of years; when it becomes infertile, the gardens are abandoned and eventually the grass takes over.) But on the ridges above Tapini there are good stands of foothill forest. It is a continuation of the lowland tropical rain forests, festooned with lianas and epiphytic plants, and it covers the lower slopes up to a height of about 4,000 feet.

I climbed up one steep ridge to enter this forest. At first I had great difficulty moving through the tangle of vines, spiky shrubs and thin saplings. This was only the front of secondary growth which fringed the forest. Once through that, walking was a bit easier, although there was still some dense undergrowth. Like many mountain ridges, the crest was almost knife-edged—barely two feet wide—and the sides dropped away so steeply that I could hold on to the topmost branches of trees whose roots were far down the slope.

There were a great many birds about, but the foliage was so thick that it was almost impossible to see them. Underfoot, the ground was alive with small skinks scuttling through the leaf litter. I watched them poking beneath the leaves for small spiders, weevils and other insects. Occasionally one would emerge with a cricket or moth in its mouth, and would bash the insect on the ground to soften it before eating it.

One very large tree with buttress roots straddled the crest of the ridge. This was the first of the big trees that make up the true rain forest. When I reached the top of the ridge, the view was obscured by leaves, but there were a couple of trees leaning against each other and I climbed them to

Feathered Extravaganza

In 1898 the English ornithologist R. B. Sharpe published the first comprehensive study of bird of paradise species. It was illustrated with colour lithographs by W. Hart, seven of which are shown here. It is a testament to Sharpe's achievement that only six new species have since been discovered, making 42 in all. Of the total, 36 are unique to New Guinea.

Most live in the lowland and mid-mountain forests, although some—like the brown sickle-bill bird of paradise (opposite page, bottom left)—range to 10,000 feet. The flamboyant, highly-prized plumage is exclusive to males, who display it in elaborate courtship dances. The Emperor of Germany bird of paradise (opposite page, bottom right) ends his dance hanging upside down and waving his fully spread tail. Others, including the King of Saxony bird of paradise (opposite page, top left) bounce and swing on tall vines.

BLACK-BILLED SICKLE-BILL BIRD OF PARADISE

BLUE BIRD OF PARADISE

PRINCESS STEPHANIE'S BIRD OF PARADISE

KING OF SAXONY BIRD OF PARADISE

TWELVE-WIRED BIRD OF PARADISE

BROWN SICKLE-BILL BIRD OF PARADISE

EMPEROR OF GERMANY BIRD OF PARADISE

look out over the crest of the canopy. From my perch I could see all the way from the coastline, shimmering in the haze of the midday heat, up to where great banks of white cumulus clouds were gathering behind the mountain summits high above. To the north-east, clouds already obscured the summit of Mount Albert Edward, one of the easier mountains to climb in Papua New Guinea. To the east the farthest ridges disappeared into the blue distance and in a valley a short way off I could see the silvery line of a fast-flowing stream, too far away to hear. But it was the view to the west that really captured my interest, for I could see the forest sweeping up the side of a broad valley right to the tree line at about 12,000 feet. Even from this distance I could detect changes in the colour and texture of the forest as it got higher.

Above 4,000 feet, the big buttress-rooted trees of the lowland rain forest begin to give way to oaks, marking the start of the cooler mid-mountain forests. Oak dominates the lower half of the mid-mountain forest, and beech the upper. At about 9,000 feet, conifers take over, becoming thinner and smaller the higher up they are. Above 12,000 feet, where few trees will grow, are the alpine grasslands.

These altitudinal zones are particularly clear on Mount Albert Edward. A track, used mainly by local people who often pass along it on mountain wallaby hunts, leads from the valley at Woitape to the summit. Where the track passes through mid-mountain forest, you could be forgiven for thinking that the trees belong more to a north temperate zone than a tropical country—oaks (*Lithocarpus*), chestnuts (*Castanopsis*), the southern beech (*Nothofagus*) and conifers (*Podocarpus*). But the birds are nothing like those you might find in a temperate country. Among them are different mountain species of birds of paradise, including the velvet-black Princess Stephanie's bird of paradise and the brown, long-tailed Meyer's sickle-bill, with its strange machine-gun-like call. These exotic creatures are part of the character of the mountain wilderness and when I see them I am content, knowing that I am in an area where few people go and where the wilderness is likely to remain.

In these high, cool forests I once came across a long-beaked echidna, *Zaglossus bruijni*, surely one of the strangest animals in the world. It lays eggs and suckles the young in its pouch. I had seen pictures of it, but really had no idea of its size and strength until I met my first one digging into some soft soil on the slopes of Mount Albert Edward. I tried to pick it up, but the animal was difficult to lift off the ground and I had to lever it up with a small sapling, grabbing a hind leg which it put out for a new foothold. The strength of this 20-pound

A mountain wallaby pauses in its search for the soft leaves, roots and fruits on which it feeds. Well equipped for hopping and jumping, this 30-inch long marsupial inhabits the mountain forests of New Guinea. Although primarily a nocturnal animal, it is also active in the early morning and can often be seen basking in the afternoon sunshine.

spiky bundle can hardly be imagined. It is about the size of a small dog but more bearlike in build with black fur that partially hides dozens of sharp spines. It has short, thick legs armed with strong claws with which it rips apart rotting logs, leaf litter and forest compost. It pokes its snout into the debris searching for earthworms, which it draws in with its long, sticky tongue.

Another animal I have seen in the mid-mountain forests—it seems common on Mount Albert Edward—is Boelen's python. It is probably the only species of python in the world that lives as high as 10,000 feet. An attractive snake, growing to more than nine feet in length and quite thick-bodied, it is satin black on top and canary yellow on the underside and has chevrons of yellow along its sides. It is not an easy animal to catch or photograph. Like all pythons, it is not poisonous; still, who wants a bite from six rows of needle-sharp teeth?

As you climb higher in these mountains, the forest changes in subtle ways: oaks and beech become less common and you start to notice conifers. Bamboo can present a real obstacle to walkers, particularly a slender-stemmed variety, *Nastus productus*, which grows at an astonishing rate, encircling shrubs and trees, snaking across paths and intertwining to form an almost impenetrable latticework. Even with a bushknife, it can take hours to get through a mere hundred yards. A friend of mine, when climbing Mount Victoria, took two whole days to force his way through a particularly thick belt of this bamboo.

At between 9,000 and 10,000 feet you enter the mist forest, so called because it is a cold, grey world where the tree-tops are often swathed in clouds for many days of the year. Here the trees, predominantly conifers, are less dense, and you begin to find shrubs related to myrtle, cranberry and huckleberry. Many of the trees are festooned with mosses, ferns and orchids, and I have counted ten different species of orchid on the branches of a single fallen tree. Some were masses of tiny *Bulbophyllum* with beautiful starry flowers. In some species, the flowers remain open only for two or three hours before they wither and die.

The mist forest is dangerous walking country, for in many places the tree roots grow above the ground, snaking and intertwining to form a precarious, moss-covered platform. You have to be very careful when you are picking a way across these interlaced roots: one false step could mean a drop of some distance and perhaps a broken leg.

Above the mist forests, as the trees become gnarled and stunted, shrubs are dominant. Myrtles and rhododendrons grow quite densely in places. The rich glowing reds, oranges and yellows of the rhododendrons brighten an otherwise grey and green vista—grey from the cloud and green from the mosses and shrubs. Higher still, at about 12,000 feet, the trees disappear altogether, and the woody thickets of shrubs are more spread out, interspersed with alpine grasses and ferns.

Bare outcrops of black rock and grass spangled with bright flowers like daisies and buttercups dominate the summit of Mount Albert Edward. It rains often at this altitude, and walking through the tussocky grass soon wets you to the thighs. There are also swamps, freezing cold streams and alpine lakes of all sizes. Some friends of mine saw a pair of Salvadori's teal on one of these lakes, patrolling back and forth in front of a small waterfall. Salvadori's teal is a fairly common duck high in the mountains, although it is rarely seen at lower altitudes.

Actually, Mount Albert Edward has two summits, separated by a low saddle. From the East Dome you get a marvellous view: on a clear morning you can see both coasts, about 120 miles apart. To the north is real mountaineering country: sheer rock faces, narrow chimneys, plunging slopes and streams cascading down through gullies for thousands of feet before suddenly flattening out towards the coastline. In the opposite direction, the isolated, flat-topped massif of Mount Yule dominates the view. This thickly forested mountain, 10,800 feet high, rises like a great blockhouse and is commonly used as a landmark by aircraft pilots. To the east and to the west, a great confusion of moun-

A strong wind lifts early morning mist out of the valleys and over the slopes of Mount Wilhelm, in the Bismarck Range of Papua New Guinea.

tains and valleys stretches away as far as the eye can see.

The temperature on the mountain tops often goes down to freezing point, with overnight frost and ice. On cloudy days the ice lasts in the shady places until midday. The air at this altitude has been described as cool and exhilarating, but in my experience it is raining more often than not and a prolonged spell in this cold, driving rain can be very trying. Yet I would never miss the experience of sitting on mountain tops watching the morning mist sweep towards me, like a waterfall rolling upwards. I have watched great banks of cloud in a valley spill over a ridge like a line of stampeding white chargers. I have seen the first light of dawn striking the sheer cliffs on the north side of Mount Victoria, making them glow and sparkle with gold flashes where shiny surfaces in the rock reflected the sun.

In such steep, wet mountains as those which form the axis of this island it is almost inevitable that there will be waterfalls everywhere. In Papua New Guinea we do not have the highest or the widest, but I should think we would be in the running for having a larger number of waterfalls than any area of similar size in the world. You can see at least one from almost any vantage point in the mountains. They provide a habitat for an infinite variety of ferns and mosses, and you can usually find some of the country's many species of begonias on the spray-drenched rocks.

It is noticeable that few birds are found near the waterfalls. My theory for this is that the falling water makes too much noise for the birds to tell when danger is near. Soaring birds are an exception, because waterfalls generate upward air currents which are good for soaring. Along the Snake river valley in the Morobe District, where there is a large waterfall dropping in cascades down a very narrow gorge, I have watched whistling eagles get a lift which sends them rocketing up to great heights from which they can survey the whole valley. And at Rouna Falls, about 26 miles from Port Moresby, there has been a pair of brahminy kites in the vicinity for at least ten years. I still see them now and again, sailing out from the forest, circling above the falls and catching an upward current that takes them up and over the edge of the Varirata escarpment in half a dozen spiralling turns.

Some waterfalls drop from a sharp ledge in a screen of white water and disappear into sinkholes, formed where the roof of an underground cave has collapsed. This creates a funnel of roaring sound; after heavy rains the noise can be deafening. I remember exploring a sinkhole in the Chimbu Province of the central highlands. A small stream fell into the hole at one point, splashed across some rocks and disappeared into the porous limestone floor. It was amazing what volume of sound came from the water falling into this miniature colosseum.

Depending on the size of the original cave, sinkholes can be 300 or more feet deep and hundreds of feet across. Usually they have vertical or even undercut sides so that it is impossible to get into them, but this particular one was quite small, about 60 feet deep and easy to climb into. I had gone there to record the cave paintings on the walls. There are many sinkholes and caves in Papua New Guinea with prehistoric paintings, usually representing ceremonial designs or tribal garbs in striking earth colours of red and yellow, white lime and black soot.

About 45 miles inland from Port Moresby there are two extensive cave systems which I have explored. The entrance to both these caves is a jagged hole in the rocks. Just inside you are greeted with the usual squeaks of the bats and are duly christened with their droppings. Swift-lets flit past you as you squelch through pungent, ankle-deep guano. Hard, wet clay and smooth, slippery limestone are a danger underfoot. There is sufficient light filtering into the cave entrance to let you see a short way. On the floor close to the entrance are round holes an inch across. These are the tunnels of the so-called bird-eating spiders which, strangely enough, seldom if ever catch birds although they can overcome weak or helpless ones. The tunnels are sometimes sunk to a depth of three feet, although generally they are about half that length. The thinnest film of silk lines the tunnel and spans the top of the hole, pro-viding a form of trip-wire system that alerts the spider to an approaching cockroach, beetle or gecko. On my last visit I could see one spider inside its hole, waiting for a victim to tread on a silken thread.

Going deeper into the caves with a torch you find fewer animals, but some of them are decidedly strange. One creature I have come across is a leech which looks like an albino, with its pale pink, almost white body and a pink head and sucker. These leeches apparently feed on the blood of birds and bats. It was while crawling through one of the winding tun-nels inside these caves that I met another rather startling animal. It was *Scutigera*, a most unusual centipede which is sometimes called a hairy nanny. This name, I feel, with its nursery connotations, hardly fits an animal that is more like a child's nightmare. Its body is suspended between two rows of incredibly long, delicate legs. Unlike the common centipede, which has 21 to 31 body segments, *Scutigera* has only 15, with 15 pairs of legs. Those who do not like scuttling creatures would do well to avoid the *Scutigera*. When it is disturbed it streaks away in such a hurry that it often drops a leg or two as it goes. Perhaps it gets out of step? The *Scutigera* is also called the bug killer—with better reason, for it eats cockroaches, crickets, flies and other small insects. It pounces and enfolds its victims in a tangle of legs. The specimens I saw were a pale, gingery-red colour and at least four inches long. These are among the larger *Scutigera* known. One inch is an average length for the common species found in most temperate countries.

Almost as strange are the spider-like amblipygids or tailless whip scorpions. I have found them in caves and also under logs and rocks in the forest. It is no wonder that some people, who would scream if a cockroach ran over them, hesitate to enter caves when such creatures as this may be lurking there. The tailless whip scorpion is related to the spiders and, like them, has four pairs of legs and a flattened body. That is about as far as the resemblance goes. It has what looks like an extra pair of legs which are really pincers, flexed inwards and lined with sharp spines on the inside. These leg-like pincers function as traps, clamping prey in their serrated edges. The scorpion's long, whip-like front legs move around continually, searching for enemies as well as for prey. If prey is detected, the scorpion moves with lightning speed to capture it. If it detects an enemy, the scorpion moves away just as speedily to the protection of a crevice.

The tunnel I was following narrowed and ended at an underground stream. There was a three-foot eel in the water. No doubt the stream ran above ground for some of its length and the eel had probably followed it in from outside. It was blackish in colour and looked like the common long-finned eel, but I had no net and the knowledge that it has sharp teeth deterred me from grabbing it by hand to identify it. The stream was deep and the eel soon disappeared under a ledge.

As I turned to retrace my steps I noticed that even at this depth, about 400 feet down, there were swiftlets flying around. Although it was pitch dark they found their way by sonar, emitting loud clicking noises which reverberated off the walls.

Often, while threading my way through underground tunnels, I have heard the dull rumble of a river that has carved itself a subterranean course. It is quite uncanny the way even sizeable rivers can just disappear in limestone country. The Tagari river is a case in point. This river has its origins in the many small streams which bubble up from the marsh and pour out of the limestone cliffs of the remote Lavani valley. When I was in the Southern Highlands collecting fossils, I visited a mission station set beside the Tagari. At this point along its course the river had become so wide that the only way to cross it was by canoe. Yet the mission people told me that a few miles downstream it simply disappeared. I decided to follow it. Not far beyond the place where I crossed in the mission's canoe, the river became narrower and more boisterous, tumbling between limestone ridges. Then, almost without warning, it dropped away into a great chaos of rocks. Beyond this point I could hear it roaring its way underground, but on the surface there was no sign of it. It does not appear again until much lower down.

Of all the wild and beautiful mountain valleys in Papua New Guinea, my favourite is the Lai river valley. You have to drive for about two hours from Mount Hagen, in the Western Highlands, past a big Baptist mission and on through forest and a few villages to reach the edge of the valley. The first time I went there I had to look around several times to take it all in. The sides of the valley, clad in colourful shrubs and grasses, drop down so steeply that they almost form a gorge. Hundreds of feet below, the river tumbles and splashes over glistening boulders. There is a plateau on the far side of the valley and beyond that a high range of sharp-crested mountains fringed with trees. In both directions you can see dozens of tributaries falling down between spurs of the plateau.

It was a textbook example of a heavily dissected plateau with many streams joining to make the river, only here it was more dramatic and colourful than any textbook could make it. The sharp outlines of the plateau, the steep green walls of the valley, the backdrop of high cliffs, the silvery river below all combined to imprint this wild scene on my mind. I felt I could have watched all day to see its different moods. It was bathed in sunlight when I arrived, but swooping down along the valleys upstream was a great billowing mass of white mist, followed by a wall of almost black rain clouds. Before I left, still in bright sunlight, the first ball of mist was close upon me and the wall of black was lighted by a dramatic display of lightning. Cracks of thunder shook the air and seemed to vibrate around me as I hurried back to my Land Rover. I drove back very slowly along the narrow track towards Mount Hagen as the darkness gathered. That maze of deep valleys has remained in my memory as one of the wildest landscapes I have ever seen.

The Descending Waters

Lying just south of the Equator and exposed for ten months of the year to moisture-bearing winds, New Guinea is one of the largest constantly wet areas in the world. Annual rainfall is rarely less than 60 inches and in some regions is often more than 160 inches.

From December to April the island feels the force of the north-west monsoons; from May to October the south-east trade winds prevail. In both cases warm, moisture-laden air is forced upwards by the high mountain ranges. The air cools in its ascent, gathering into billowing folds of cumulo-nimbus cloud that unleash heavy rainstorms as the moisture condenses. Water courses down the mountainsides in a spider's web of streams and torrents that merge into more than 20 large rivers.

During the first stage of their descent to the sea, the rivers gush and roar down precipitous slopes, often in waterfalls hundreds of feet high. Some of the streams disappear into saucer-shaped sinkholes to continue their course underground.

On reaching the lowland plains, the rivers take on a different character. Chocolate-coloured with their loads of sediment, most of them meander across the undulating landscape, creating an ever-shifting pattern of channels and mudbanks. Changes in the course of a meandering river are frequently marked by crescent-shaped lakes known as ox-bows. An ox-bow forms when the neck of land between each end of a river loop becomes narrowed by erosion. In time of flood the river breaches the neck, straightening its course so that a backwater is created. Silt deposited at the entrances to the backwater eventually cuts it off from the new course taken by the river and the backwater becomes a lake.

When slow-flowing rivers, such as the Hawain, reach the lowlands they deposit enormous quantities of silt; this builds up into fan-shaped deltas over which a maze of streams and channels wind to the sea. As more and more silt is dumped, the delta extends its boundaries into the ocean.

Faster flowing rivers, like the Sepik and the Fly, carry their silt more than 40 miles beyond the coastline, staining the surface with varying shades of brown. Some of the water that reaches the sea is evaporated by the sun and drawn up into the clouds that hover over the island's mountain peaks. Falling in time as rain, this water adds further volume to the descending rivers.

During the monsoon season, from December to April, rain-bearing clouds obscure the peaks of western Papua New Guinea's Karius Range from mid-morning onwards. By early afternoon, when this photograph was taken, the cloud curtain is dense enough to deluge the mountains with torrential rain.

The Nomad river on Mount Sisa, in the Southern Highlands of Papua New Guinea, plummets into a mammoth sinkhole. Flowing below ground, the river re-emerges several miles away. A typical feature of this limestone area, the sinkhole was formed when the roof of an underground cave collapsed.

At the base of a sinkhole the Jimi river carves a path through limestone in the Bismarck Range of central Papua New Guinea. The river's carving tools are the eroded boulders and pebbles it carries in its flow; when these rock fragments are swirled by the currents, they wear away or gouge out the rock.

Swollen by a sudden rainstorm, the waters of Big Wau Creek rage down the lower slopes of Mount Kaindi, in north-eastern Papua New Guinea. The Big Wau is usually no more than a gently-flowing trickle around the boulders that now are mostly submerged. But like most New Guinea streams on any afternoon during the rainy season, it can quickly turn into a foaming torrent.

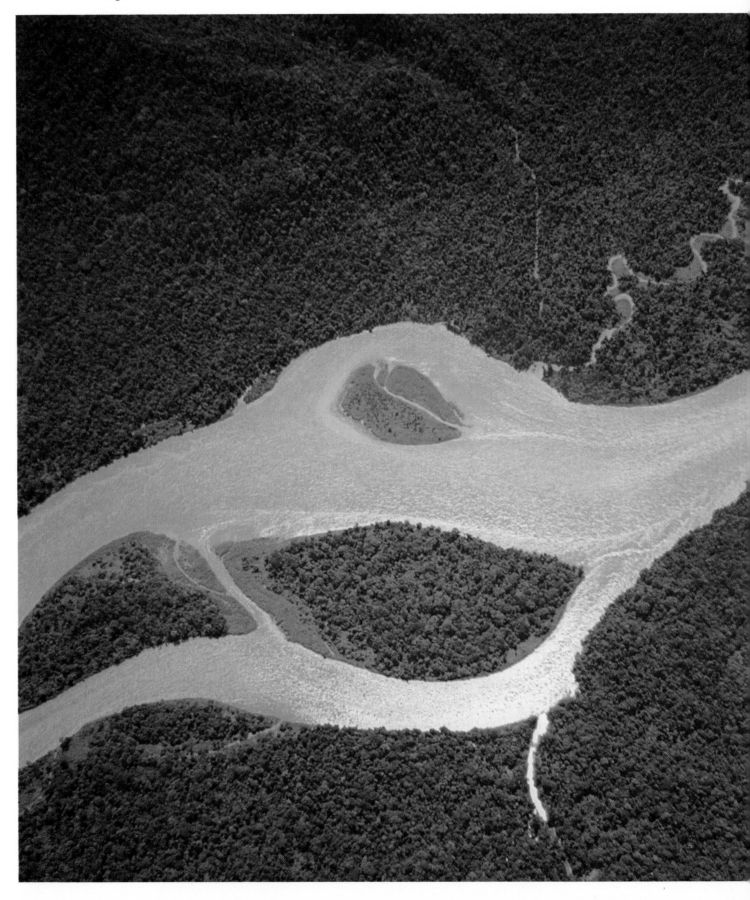

Islands of silt divide the waters of the Purari river (left) some 50 miles inland from the Papuan coast. The silt collects because the river's rapid flow has slowed abruptly as it emerges from the Eastern Highlands. Although vegetation gives the islands an air of permanence, they could be swept downstream in the next flood.

The 240-mile-long Strickland river meanders through the forest-clad lowlands of western Papua New Guinea towards its confluence with the Fly river. The crescent-shaped formation to the left of the river was once a loop of the Strickland, but was transformed into an ox-bow lake—now dry and vegetation filled—when the river changed its course.

Before emptying into the sea west of
Wewak, the Hawain river breaks up into
a network of streams and channels.
Some of the silt carried by the river is
swept away by tidal action to be
deposited along the coastline where,
gradually colonized by mangrove trees,
it extends the shore out to sea.

3/ Down the Fly River

*I know of no part of the world, the exploration
of which is so flattering to the imagination, so
likely to be fruitful in interesting results, whether
to the naturalist, the ethnologist or the geographer.*

J. BEETE JUKES/ *NARRATIVE OF THE SURVEYING VOYAGE OF H.M.S. FLY*

I stood in the doorway of the village resthouse at Golgubip, close to the
border with Irian Jaya, listening to the storm that raged violently in the
mountains above and around me. Cascades of rain beat against the
thatched roof, yet not a trickle leaked through; and although the ground
outside was drenched with racing torrents of water, I was in no danger
even of getting my feet wet, for the house, like all others in the village,
was raised on piles three feet high. The echoing roars of thunder and the
unbroken tattoo of rain overhead plainly ruled out any possibility of
sleep, so I settled down to enjoy the storm and to watch the brilliant
streaks of lightning that slashed across the night sky, illuminating the
300-foot cliffs of the Hindenburg Wall looming above the village a couple
of miles away. From a window at the back of the resthouse I caught
flashlit glimpses of swollen rivulets racing through rock gullies to swell
the flood slapping against the piles of my frail shelter. Snaking down
from the cordillera, these streams would eventually merge to form a
broader torrent—the headwaters of the mighty Fly river, known to
the local people as the Wok Feneng.

The Fly is one of Papua New Guinea's four principal rivers which rise
in the ranges of the central highlands, wind sinuous paths to north or
south through the mountains and then flow across silt plains and marshland on their journeys to the Gulf of Papua and the Bismarck Sea. The
fierce storm now feeding the convergent streams of the Fly on my side

of the range was simultaneously swelling the headwaters of the Sepik only a few miles to the north, but on the opposite face of the cordillera. And more than a hundred miles farther east other storms were possibly transforming the south-flowing Purari and the north-flowing Ramu into seething torrents as well.

I had been sent to Golgubip by the Papua New Guinea Museum in order to take a look at the spirit houses of the region. The spirit house is the traditional meeting place for initiated men of New Guinea tribes and the spot where young men undergo their secret initiation rites. Women are forbidden to enter this hallowed precinct. Inside the house are kept sacred objects, including ancient fighting shields, bones of animals, especially pigs and cuscuses, and sometimes bones of ancestors.

Having made my survey of these spirit houses, I intended to follow the course of the upper Fly on foot and by air to the point where the river emerges from the mountains to begin its long journey across the Papuan plains. I was already familiar with the lower reaches of the Fly, particularly that vast region of forested plains, swamps and lagoons known as the trans-Fly country, but I had never yet had the opportunity of exploring the magnificent upper stretches of the river where it tumbles precipitously down from the mountains.

Some time around midnight the fury of the storm abated and as the rain dissolved into a thin mist I prepared to go to bed. Flashing my torch around the bare room, I found I had company. On the walls was a miniature zoo. A miscellany of crickets, moths and beetles had found shelter here from the rain, and several house geckoes were busy stalking and eating them. Three small spiders scuttled over the floor, but having satisfied myself that they were harmless, I had no qualms about sharing my sleeping quarters with them. I might not have rested so peacefully had one of them turned out to be a bird-eating spider. Its bite is not deadly, as I can testify, having once been bitten on the foot by one. But it was certainly painful, and kept me in bed for some time with dizzy spells, nausea and a badly swollen foot.

I lay for a while listening to the roar of the waters rushing down the steep stream beds. Then I made out another faint sound—the croaking of frogs. I have always been a keen collector of reptiles and amphibians, so I hauled on my ankle boots and ventured out with a torch. I followed a village trail into the forest and was soon rewarded by the sight of frogs hopping all over the place. Males were perched prominently on rocks, leaves and the thin stems of rattan palms. Some sat boldly in the centre of the track, throat pouches pulsating to the rhythm of their individual calls. One beautiful Zweifel's frog, gleaming gold and brown in the beam of my torch, sat on a black rock, croaking away for all he was worth, intent on attracting a female. Suddenly he sensed danger and swivelled round from the waist to look at me. I kept as still as possible, trying to hold the beam steady. He really must have been keen to catch a mate for after a few moments he turned away and resumed his love calling. Slowly I backed off, searching for other species. I managed to find eight in all, mostly tree frogs of the family *Pelodryadidae* which is found in the Australia and New Guinea region. Several pairs were mating and many others were just hoping to. As I made my way back to the resthouse I became aware of small bats hawking insects up and down the trail; flicking my torch about, I counted two or three species.

The next morning was fine. Behind the village, rivulets were in full spate, dull reddish-ochre from the silt washed into them, dislodging pebbles and small boulders. From a knoll just outside Golgubip I could see the deep clefts cut in the Hindenburg Wall by these small head-streams of the upper Fly. Miniature waterfalls tumbled over the ledges into space, providing vivid evidence of the quantity of water that had been unleashed by the storm.

I spent the day visiting a number of spirit houses and making useful additions to my dossier of notes and photographs. Then, after a quieter night, I completed preparations for my journey downriver. I had made some good friends among the villagers and some half-dozen of the local men volunteered to come along as carriers. They were a picturesque crew whose sole concession to modesty was a long, curly gourd covering the penis, the tip of the gourd being attached by a cord to a cane belt. The rest of their everyday dress consisted of an assortment of bandoleers and strings, or lengths of cassowary wing quills. A couple of them also sported facial adornment: a pair of rhinoceros-beetle horns inserted in holes pierced clean through the nose.

Our objective on the first day was the village of Olsobip, ten miles away to the south-west. Olsobip lies at an altitude of only 1,500 feet, and since we were some 5,000 feet up in the mountains, the descent would be sharp. We set out along a track that passed through a splendid stretch of mid-mountain forest, and down into the Fly river valley. Although the sun was up, the light inside the forest was so poor that I had to use a time exposure for photographs. But I had little chance to admire the scenery for soon the path sloped steeply downwards and became treacherous. Sodden, moss-covered roots snaked out across the trail, while in other places the hazard was smooth, wet limestone. At one

A bush-cricket hangs precariously from a forest leaf while it sheds the hard outer skin it has outgrown. Eventually the newly moulted and vulnerable insect will hide itself in the foliage until its new outer skin has become hardened. But several further moults have to be undergone before maturity is reached.

point I went skating off into thin air, landing heavily on my bottom, to the enormous glee of the carriers. They were equally amused when I stepped across what seemed to be a flat stretch of white sand. A few sticks had been placed over the surface as a bridge but one or two were missing. As I put my foot down into the apparently firm sand, I discovered that below its shallow surface was deep mud. Roaring with laughter, two of the carriers hauled me out. My leg was encrusted with slime but I sustained no injury, except to my dignity!

It was hard going and I was relieved when we came to the edge of a large clearing and took a rest. To accustom our eyes to the blinding sunlight after the intense forest gloom, we stood in the shade of the trees or sat down on limestone rocks beside the track. One of the carriers seated on a rock opposite me seemed totally unaware of two skinks that were chasing each other around his legs. Seen in shade, they were dark grey above with white and black stripes along the sides; but when they stopped in a patch of sunlight their bodies glittered with rainbow hues. A grasshopper jumped on to the carrier's leg and when he bent to swat it, the lizards bolted under the rock. I could see plenty of others, though, dashing through the grass and under the leaf litter, or else basking in the sun. While we rested, a cloud of brilliant yellow butterflies, members of the genus *Catopsilia*, fluttered into the glade and many settled on us. They also seemed to be on a journey for they soon drifted on.

As we were about to start, a pair of eclectus parrots circled high above us. Flying over the treetops, these birds appear simply as black silhouettes against the glaring blue of the sky—but in fact both male and female are strikingly coloured. The male's body is mostly bright green, the leading edge of the wings and primaries being deep blue and the sides of the body and underwing coverts scarlet. The female is, if anything, clad in more brilliant plumage, contrary to the norm among bird species. She is rich red all over except for a broad, violet-blue band across the breast which joins a narrow band of the same colour across the mantle. The same deep blue adorns the leading edges of wings, primaries and underwing coverts. So different are the sexes that they were once thought to be separate species.

The parrots flew about screeching noisily and although I was sure that there was a nest near by, there was no time to look for it. The carriers were impatient to reach Olsobip before darkness. We splashed through the Fly river at a point where the bed was a jumble of limestone rocks, and then followed a more level path, skirting what had once been

The pink flower, circular leaves and fruiting head of the oriental or sacred lotus rise above the waters of Lake Murray. The saucer-shaped surface of the fruit is spotted with protruding red seeds which can be eaten when ripe. Flower and leaf stalks grow up from a tangle of rhizomes embedded in the mud and extending over 30 feet.

garden land and was now a tangle of vines and shrubs of secondary growth. The rain forest came steeply down to the opposite bank, the upper branches of the trees being festooned with mosses, ferns, orchids and Hoya vines. After a mile or so we crossed back into the forest and temporarily lost sight of the river, which had suddenly narrowed and tumbled down a gully more than 50 feet deep. The sun was setting when we reached Olsobip—a cluster of huts nestling on a flat shelf overlooking the valley. The river here was much broader and deeper, and it foamed around massive black boulders.

Next day we took off from an airstrip outside the village to continue the journey south. The Fly river leaves the mountains and enters the Great Papuan Plateau by way of Gum Gorge, a spectacular chasm with almost perpendicular sides. The gorge is less than a mile long but disconcertingly narrow—about 300 yards across. The airstrip lies at the head of the gorge, and immediately after take-off we were flying between the sheer walls. The wing-tips of the small, single-engined plane appeared so close to the sides that I was frightened they would touch. As we raced past I got an uncomfortably close view of the mosses, grasses and small shrubs which hung by their roots from the rock face. Hoping fervently that the pilot knew his business, I forced myself to look down at the smooth, dark ribbon of the Fly, flecked with patches of silvery foam, as it bubbled through the gap.

Our flight—and my observations of the river—ended at Kiunga, about 40 miles south-west of Olsobip. From this point the Fly is navigable by cargo boat down to its mouth 500 miles away. Beyond Kiunga the mountain ranges tail off into low ridges and then merge with the grey-green of rain forest and plain; and across this flat landscape I could see the river, now much wider and swollen by other tributaries, meandering due south towards the sea. I had covered about 50 miles of the 800-mile-long Fly—a relatively short distance, admittedly, but I had had an incomparable glimpse of the river at its wildest and most majestic.

It was difficult to equate the turbulent torrents of the mid-mountain forests with the tranquil, evenly flowing current farther down where the Fly joins the Strickland, another almost equally powerful river which crashes down from mountains more than 10,000 feet high in the Western Highlands. This region is sparsely populated owing to the presence of malaria; and because there is little hunting, animals that are considered rare in other parts of Papua New Guinea, such as cassowaries, wallabies, bandicoots and goura pigeons, are common in this splendid wilderness.

One heavily forested area surrounds Lake Murray, some 40 miles north of the Fly-Strickland confluence. When I last visited this lake the water was high and the surface liberally dotted with blue, white and pink water-lilies, each flower about six inches in diameter. The lake is tranquil and colourful by day, but can take on a sinister quality at night when crocodiles are abroad, hunting for food, their eyes glinting brilliantly red or orange-red in the beam of a torch. Nothing reacts more self-consciously than a crocodile when he suddenly finds he is not alone, under the scrutiny of an interested naturalist. A flick of the tail, a swirl of water, and he disappears. A minute later he rises to the surface with only his nostrils and eyes showing, and returns the gaze. Once I met a crocodile in one of the beds of water-lilies to be found on the lake. I was in a canoe, and as the boat silently drifted closer and closer, he continued to eye me. Finally, when I was only ten yards away, he dived under in a great flurry, sending water-lilies flying through the air.

It is possible to gauge a crocodile's dimension roughly by the size of its eyes. Wading in the shallows at night, I have sometimes crept up and grabbed hold of young, inexperienced crocodiles. They are delightful little creatures and all they do is let out "giak, giak" squawks of alarm until they are released. But when a crocodile becomes slightly older and measures about three feet, it is more of a handful, shaking itself vigorously in its efforts to wriggle free and escape to deeper waters.

Jaws agape, an estuarine crocodile thrashes through silt-laden river waters in southern Papua New Guinea. The larger of two species of crocodile found in New Guinea, the estuarine may reach a length of as much as 23 feet. Both species feed primarily on fish and small animals that come within their grasp and the estuarine will also prey on man.

Any crocodile that is more than three feet long is to be avoided, because its bite is quite dangerous.

Lake Murray contains two species—the estuarine crocodile and the New Guinea crocodile. The former, which is known to reach lengths of up to 23 feet, is a man-eater, although usually it preys on fish or on animals that come to the water to drink. The New Guinea species, which is usually not much more than 14 feet long, feeds almost exclusively on fish. A favourite meal of both species is the Jardine's barramundi, a giant fish weighing upwards of 50 pounds. The barramundi makes an annual migration from Lake Murray to the sea, a journey of more than 300 miles, to spawn either in the estuary of the Fly or off the coasts. Its flesh is prized as much by the local villagers as by the crocodiles and a variety of methods are used to catch the fish. Sometimes the villagers use a simple hook and line; sometimes they shoot it with a bow and arrow or spear it from a canoe.

Apart from the crocodiles, many other creatures are active in and around the waters of Lake Murray at night. Strolling along its edge with a powerful torch, I saw frogs hopping over leaf litter, and a brown tree snake glided slowly through some near-by branches. Rainbow fish, their flanks striped in bright green and mauve, swam close to the shore, feeding on algae and insects, and water beetles darted on the surface of the water. There was a soft plopping noise. Perhaps a frog had jumped into the water, although it could just as well have been a Javan file snake. This stocky, harmless snake is common in the swampy, lower-Fly regions and in other parts of the Western and Gulf Provinces. It measures six to eight feet long and has a loose skin that feels like a coarse file. Out of the water it looks ludicrously unattractive; if held by the mid-section, the body contents sag to either end. But in its natural environment of water it is a remarkably graceful and powerful swimmer. I once saw a file snake crossing a fast-flowing stream. Any other snake would have been carried helplessly downstream, but this one moved easily just below the surface, coming up occasionally to breathe, and reached the opposite shore without difficulty.

On my walk along the shores of Lake Murray I spotted, almost within hand's reach, a small honeyeater fast asleep on a branch, its feathers so puffed out that it looked like a round ball of fluff. Like the honeyeater, most of the birds in the area are diurnal, but there were enough strange calls to give away the presence of a few nocturnal species, and I could distinguish the soft ventriloquial "oom, oom, oom" of the great Papuan frogmouth, a bird of New Guinea and north Australia which resembles a large nightjar. The frogmouth catches insects on the wing, and I have even seen one chasing small bats.

South of Lake Murray, as the Fly and the Strickland join forces to form a single watercourse and approach the sea, the banks get higher and the channel wider. Now the river moves more slowly, its surface opaque from the quantity of brown and reddish silt it is carrying. You cannot see your hand six inches underwater. About 150 miles from its mouth the Fly-Strickland is almost a mile wide, yet navigation is far from easy, for the channel is dotted with large mud islands, some of them five miles long. The flow of the mighty river slackens even more as it meets the tidal pressure of the sea and spreads wide around a multitude of mud banks and islets. The mouth of the estuary is about 60 miles wide and the silt-laden waters reach out some 45 miles into the Gulf of Papua, where even ten miles offshore the water is a mere 200 feet deep.

Barely-covered mud banks, floating logs and *nypa* palms are constant hazards to shipping; but far more dangerous is the tidal wave or "bore" that races up the lower Fly on the first three days of every new moon. The incoming high tide generated by the moon's gravitational pull forces its way through the estuary, since its pressure is far greater than that of the river flowing in the opposite direction. A six-foot wall of water, sometimes reinforced by smaller waves, rushes upriver as far as the junction with the Strickland, causing much destruction along the banks.

One explorer of New Guinea, Jack Hides, had a disastrous encounter with the bore during a journey to the Fly-Strickland area in 1937. On his return, he was travelling by canoe with two natives, Nou and Bije, and a sick companion, David Lyall. As they paddled downstream they heard above the roar of wind and rain, a sustained rumbling sound. Realizing what it might be, they scrambled ashore and carried Lyall to the highest point on the bank; and while Nou stayed with him, Hides and Bije made preparations to save their canoe and equipment. They only had time to brace the canoe by sticking the paddles in the mud. Within minutes a wall of white water struck with such force that the canoe and both men were sent tumbling upstream. Gasping for breath, Hides swam for the shore; but the power of the tide carried him even farther upriver.

When eventually he came within reach of land he was prevented from climbing to higher ground by a fringing thicket of lawyer vines with their notorious recurved barbs, and he had to clamber along the slippery banks until he got back to the spot where Nou and Lyall were waiting. Hides then levered up the lawyer vines with a long pole so that they could crawl under for shelter from the wind and rain. They spent a miserable night, plagued by mosquitoes and sandflies, worrying about Bije—presumed to have drowned—and the loss of all food, equipment and means of transport. Next morning, however, Bije reappeared and they used his sheath-knife to construct a frail raft on which they struggled downstream. They reached Daru, but the journey had been too much for Lyall. He died a day or two later.

My own exploration of the rivers and lakes in southern Papua New Guinea has been extensive. I have travelled the lowland waterways by motor boat or native canoe, and swum through crystal-clear streams observing many fascinating fish and marine insects. My hunts for interesting animals and plants have taken me on several occasions to the so-called Lake district. This extensive and fascinating region, situated a little way north of the mouth of the Fly river, comprises many beautiful lakes and lagoons sprinkled with green islands and fed by the Aramia river. On one of my journeys, I arranged with some local canoe owners to make a crossing of Balimo Lagoon, the largest of them all.

It was a marvellous way to travel. Not content to be a mere passenger, I joined a team of five native paddlers in their 30-foot canoe and, after some initial trepidation, found myself doing surprisingly well. The canoe looked very unstable, and since the paddlers had to stand up in line, I was worried about keeping my balance. Wisely, they placed me in the middle and before long I managed to pick up the dipping and pulling rhythm of the man in front. When the experts saw that I was keeping time, they stepped up the pace and soon we were flashing through the water. When we slowed down or stopped, I was able to look around. At one spot a couple of little terns flew off as we drifted towards their resting place at the edge of the lagoon. Overhead two whistling eagles soared high on air currents; plumed egrets waded in the shallows and red-combed jacanas skipped lightly over the water-lilies. A little black cormorant was diving for fish in a patch of clear water. It was one of those idyllic moments when life seems perfect—the sun shining, the paddles quietly dipping, the birds busy hunting, all against the bright green background of grass and bush and the neat thatched houses of Balimo village nestling near the water's edge.

In this largely unspoiled region I never cease to be amazed at the profusion of plant and freshwater animal life, and almost every trip has provided some reward. I once hired a motor boat to take me up the Kikori river on a visit to local villages, where I hoped to catalogue and collect traditional wood carvings and other local artifacts. My starting point,

A newly hatched New Guinea snapper turtle clambers over the other eggs deposited in the muddy earth of the egg chamber. As it slowly reaches maturity, the baby tortoise will develop the prominent snout, strong jaws and aggressive nature that give this freshwater reptile its colloquial name.

the town of Kikori, lies on the western fringes of the huge Purari delta, where some of the surrounding country has been altered by coconut plantations and other forms of agriculture. We were soon in the shadow of secondary forest. Draperies of vines drooped down from the tops of trees into the water, their leaves rising and falling with the tide. At one place we brushed past a curtain of brilliant scarlet flowers of the D'Albertis' creeper, first described by Luigi D'Albertis, the Italian explorer, in the 1870s. The creeper is also known, appropriately, as the "flame of the forest". It hung in great cascades from the trees; many of the blooms had dropped off and were floating on the surface of the river.

As we swung wide to pass through a channel between two mud banks, I noticed the tracks of some Fly river turtles that had dragged themselves up on to high ground to deposit their eggs. Motioning to my boatman to pull in, I jumped out to take a look at the nests. Immediately a large monitor lizard raced off into the thicket. It had been digging into a turtle's nest and had already eaten several eggs, leaving about 20 more unbroken. They were roughly twice the size of a golf ball, with tough, parchment-like shells. The nest was about a foot down in the silted mud. Only two of the 12 visible nest sites appeared to be untouched. The others had been raided by the voracious lizards.

The Fly river turtle is an extraordinary animal that looks rather like a saltwater green turtle, except that its shell is more prominently domed; and instead of consisting of horny plates, it is covered with leathery skin. The nostrils are extended into two tubes, placed close together so that when the turtle rises to the surface to breathe only the very nostril tips need protrude above water. This turtle possesses flippers like a sea turtle and lives in the brackish waters of river estuaries from the Gulf Province through to the south coast of Irian Jaya. Its food consists largely of the fruits of estuarine mangroves. In spite of the depredation of the nests by monitor lizards and other predators, the Fly river turtle population remains fairly stable.

After padding some fresh silt over the unbroken eggs, I clambered back into the motor boat and we headed upstream past heavier forest. Later I landed on a small island outcrop of limestone covered with vine-festooned trees, bamboo thickets and many smaller plants. On one high, straight wall of limestone I was delighted to find a rare species of begonia which I wanted for the University gardens at Port Moresby. Unlike the slightly crescent-shaped leaves of some begonias, these leaves were almost circular, each four to eight inches across, and growing on a short stem. There must have been a hundred plants on this single wall. Some had small, bright pink flowers on a tall stem standing out from the disc-like leaves. So as not to disturb the group too much I collected only a few samples at random and then resumed the journey.

After cruising upstream for another half hour, we reached the end of the secondary forest with its tangle of heavy undergrowth, and landed for a picnic lunch in a stretch of beautiful primary forest with a high canopy and open floor thickly carpeted with leaves. In a stroll after lunch, I wandered among trees with enormous, flanged buttress roots. Two such giants were clearly doomed to die in the ever-tightening embrace of strangler figs. Between the buttresses, heaps of fallen leaves had collected and tunnels had been burrowed through them and down into the tree roots by small animals. Unfortunately there was no time to linger, since our destination, the village of Barakiwa, lay some considerable distance upriver. But the discovery of the rare begonias had been enough to make my day.

The underwater life of the rivers and lakes is just as interesting to me as that which can be seen above water. Freshwater animals have too often been studied by hauling samples out for study above, and I feel there is a great deal to be learned by exploring with a snorkel or aqualung. At the edge of the lowlands, only 1,500 feet above sea level, there are many streams alive with fascinating fish and insect species. On several occasions I have ventured into Ei Creek, about 40 miles inland from Port Moresby, with a mask and snorkel. Once I kicked up a little sand from the bottom, and schools of small, gaily coloured rainbow fish darted in to feed on any microscopic life that might have been uncovered. Water beetles, dragonfly larvae and worms moved freely about among the fronds of water weeds lodged in the rocks. Another day I watched a giant water bug with pincer-like forelegs attack and kill a large tadpole. These insects are about four inches in length and are such expert swimmers that even fish are not safe from their rapacious assaults. Once a year, around the beginning of the wet season, adult water bugs embark on a migration flight. They invade lighted areas of towns in their thousands, but why they do so and where they go remain mysteries.

For lake exploration an aqualung affords more scope than a mask and snorkel. Sitting on the bottom of one lagoon near Port Moresby, I have enjoyed a ringside view of many an underwater drama. Once I watched a school of tilapia—a food fish introduced from Africa. They are mouth breeders. The male fans a depression in the sand where the female lays her eggs. Then he scoops the eggs into his mouth and shelters them until they hatch. Only a few feet away from me, a freshwater crab sifted food from the silt on the lake bed, and long-armed shrimps scuttled to and fro, hiding in crevices in the banks whenever they felt threatened. A New Guinea snapper turtle floated into my field of vision. Its head and black upper shell were invisible above the water but from below I could admire the bright scarlet and off-yellow tints of its plastron.

The turtle dived and came to within a yard of me before sensing danger; without pausing, it turned and dashed away. It is surprising how rapidly an animal can move when threatened, and on this particular occasion I discovered that this was true of myself as well. As I turned to look in the opposite direction, my heart skipped a few beats; for there, barely 20 feet away, was a crocodile. It was probably not more than six feet long, but it looked much bigger underwater. The shock was enough to send me shooting to the surface so fast that I seemed to be walking with my flippers. Then I sped for the shore, content to call it a day.

NATURE WALK / Over the Astrolabes

From the top of a hillock about 20 miles inland from Port Moresby, the photographer Eric Lindgren and I gazed eastwards across an undulating savannah woodland which lay at the mouth of the Rouna Valley. The valley was set between two ridges of the Astrolabe Range, a low mountain chain fringing the foothills of the high Owen Stanley Range which forms part of the backbone of Papua New Guinea.

Eric and I had come here to begin a two-day walk that would take us through a number of different vegetation zones ranging from these savannah woodlands to primary rain forest. We were hoping to observe the rich and varied plant and wildlife of each habitat.

Stretching out before us in the foreground was a good cover of eucalypts, although where the trees grew sparsely, high *Themeda* and *Imperata*, or so-called blady grass, covered the ground. Above the surrounding country projected the 300-foot eminences known as Twin Peaks. Ahead of us the Rouna Valley rose gradually to meet the escarpment of the Sogeri Plateau on the Astrolabe Range. At the apex of the valley, the Rouna Falls poured the floodwaters of the Laloki river in a

solid curtain of white foam to a mist-shrouded pool below. Flanking the valley to the north were the beetling cliffs of a long spur of the Astrolabe Range known as Hombrom Bluff, after a French naturalist.

A little to the south of the bluff, the slightly less precipitous slopes of the Varirata spur tumbled down in black agglomerate ridges, covered mostly in savannah vegetation but interspersed with semi-deciduous rain forest. The small, outlying peak of Mount Hiwick stood like a sentinel at the gateway to the valley.

Final objective

Our plan was to go up the Rouna Valley as far as the falls and then turn south and climb 1,500 feet up the Varirata spur, at the top of which we would camp for the night. The following day we intended to cross the rolling Sogeri Plateau, making for Ower's Corner, a large patch of once cultivated land that has gone to waste. From there we would descend to join the Kokoda Trail and, after fording the Goldie river, push on to our final objective—the Imita Ridge.

We left our hillock, aiming towards a swamp that was surrounded by trees and shrubs. An extended rainy season had left it

still waterlogged, although soon it would be a dry clay-pan. Candle bushes, their yellow-flowering heads reminiscent of glowing candles, overhung the edge of the swamp, and tall eucalypt and paperbark trees circled its perimeter.

A flock of white-headed stilts, disturbed by our intrusion, flew into

FLOCK OF WHITE-HEADED STILTS

the air, their beautiful black and white plumage emphasized by the pale pink of their trailing legs. As they circled above us we could hear the soft, flute-like cadences of their calls. We saw other birds, including a flock of noisy rainbow lorikeets and two white-throated butcher birds which chortled from the crown of a high Boroko gum tree.

Moving on, we climbed a rise of matted grasses and vines leading towards the high bank of the Laloki river, which courses through the Rouna Valley. A narrow gorge cut through the opposite bank, and at the entrance to the gorge a tiny waterfall cascaded behind a screen of shrubbery and vines.

THE TWIN PEAKS

The gorge was no more than 30 feet wide, but the bank on which we stood dropped away too sharply for us to climb down to the waterfall. As we looked about we saw several flowering vines draped thickly over the grass and shrubs. Among them was the butterfly pea vine, *Clitoria ternatea*, a slender climber whose flowers range in colour from pale to dark blue and which have a life span of only one day.

We headed along the bank of the Laloki towards the Rouna Falls. Dotted here and there among the eucalypts were cycads, *Cycas circinalis*. These plants, reminiscent of ancient tree ferns, are primitive gymnosperms that have remained almost unchanged for about 200

YOUNG FRONDS OF A CYCAD

BUTTERFLY PEA VINE

million years. Most were about four feet high, although a few specimens grew as high as 12 feet. The cycads are often scorched when the natives burn the grass in the dry season, but the plants soon bring forth a new crown of fronds which resembles a bunch of plumes.

Watching our progress and occasionally dashing out to catch flying insects were two rainbow bee-eaters, *Merops ornatus*. These birds are aptly named, for their plumage has the most striking range of rich colours—rusty reds, oranges, yellows, greens and blues, with streaks of black for contrast. There are two races of bee-eaters around Port Moresby: one is a resident breeding population, the other a migrant one which disappears in the wet season. Naturalists know the latter migrates to Australia but until more birds have been ringed and recaptured we will not be able to trace their route.

Into the oven

Out in the open savannah the heat beat down and reflected off the tall grass around us. We felt as if we were in an oven and even the light breeze did little to relieve our

A PAIR OF RAINBOW BEE-EATERS

A COLLAPSED AMORPHOPHALLUS

discomfort as we pushed on towards the falls. After a while we rested in the shade of a dense thicket. Suddenly our nostrils were assailed by the terrible stench emanating from an *Amorphophallus campanulatus*. In full bloom the flower stands 18 inches high and looks like an arum lily. Reaching the end of its four-day flowering, this one had collapsed but was still giving off the characteristic smell of rotting meat which attracts pollinating insects.

We moved on and saw our first umbrella tree, *Schefflera actinophylla*. Near the falls we saw more of these distinctive trees, their spikes of red flowers projecting above the fan of leaves that radiated like the spokes of an umbrella from the end of thin branches. The flowers, too, looked like miniature umbrellas.

A LOFTY UMBRELLA TREE

The track we followed along the narrowing gorge of the Laloki river brought us within earshot of the Rouna Falls and we were soon enveloped by its thunderous roar. As we rounded the last bend we saw above us the white curtain of water of the upper section of the falls plunging 300 feet over the sharp edge of a cliff. In front of us, a lower section of the falls gushed over a pile of black boulders and crashed into a deep, grey-green pool.

Plants, kept perpetually soaked by the spray, grew in wild profusion and hordes of grasshoppers, dragon flies and other insects were much in evidence. Giant hover flies, Syrphidae, with wing spans of one and a half inches, hung almost motionless in the air, then swooped away to land on the wet rocks. The wealth of insect life was a magnet to predators such as the snake-eyed skink, *Cryptoblepharus boutonii*. One of these four-inch lizards was happily snapping up ants, while another lay sunning itself on a warm, dry rock. It

LOWER ROUNA FALLS

A GIANT HOVER FLY

A SNAKE-EYED SKINK SUNBATHING

seemed to be enjoying the heat released from the rock, for it occasionally moved along a few inches to flatten itself once more against a warmer part of the surface. This skink cannot move its eyelids, and as a result it has the fixed stare of a snake. It is rather flattened and this allows it to creep into very narrow cracks in pursuit of insect prey.

Dearth of birds

While Eric took photographs of the small-scale wildlife and I attempted to list all that we saw and photographed, it occurred to us just how few bird species seemed to be present. Besides some sparrow hawks, buzzards and swiftlets, the only others that caught our attention were three river flycatchers—often found near cascading water—and a brahminy kite, *Haliastur indus.*

This magnificent bird glided effortlessly round and round on the strong thermals caused by the rushing water of the falls, its white head contrasting sharply with its chestnut-red back, wings and breast.

A BRAHMINY KITE SOARING ON A THERMAL

Although mainly an insect and mouse-eater, it also takes fish from inland waters and will harass other birds until they release the food they have caught for themselves.

It is found not only in Papua New Guinea but also around the coasts and inland areas of India, through South-east Asia to the Solomon Islands and Australia, up to a level of about 7,500 feet. I have seen at least two of these birds in the vicinity of the Rouna Falls during the past ten years and have watched several broods of young leave the nest to find their own territories.

The afternoon was drawing on and we prepared to leave. Just before we moved off, however, Eric took several photographs of an array of small yellow butterflies gathered on a rock. Like so many flags waving about, these common grass yellows, *Eurema hecabe*, fluttered about seeking to find better drinking spots. Occasionally our activity alarmed them and they flew off, only to return one by one to resume their flag waving.

COMMON GRASS YELLOWS

A SCUTIGERA CENTIPEDE RESTING ON A LEAF

of midday often obscures the coastal view and, at the end of each dry season, the smoke from grass fires spreads a grey haze over everything. In the wet season the view is usually crystal clear in the morning, but soon after midday clouds build up and damp mists blow strongly over the escarpment. Now, however, the haze of dust rising from the savannah together with the golden glow of the sinking sun helped to mask the coast from our view.

As we climbed the steep slope of the Varirata spur of the Astrolabe Range, we entered a region that combined bushy savannah with thick monsoon rain forest. This was part of Papua New Guinea's first conservation area, the Varirata National Park, a 3,265-acre tract that offers a mixed and secure habitat to a wide range of wildlife.

I had wandered through the area before it was turned into a national park and remembered that there were several tracks, although mostly ill-defined and often petering out in a tangle of vines, saplings and fallen timbers. It was one of these tracks leading through the forest that we wished to explore once darkness had fallen.

By the time we had reached the crest of the escarpment it was late and the sun was setting. On a clear day it is possible to get a spellbinding view of the Papuan coast, from Bootless Bay in the south-east to Redscar Bay in the north-west. From the base of the escarpment to the bottom of the talus slopes, a tall forest covers the ground. There is hardly a break in the canopy of green and the trees are packed so tightly that they seem to be part of some giant cauliflower.

Beyond this forest the dry savannah woodland of the Central Province stretches to the coast. The heat

As we sat gazing out across the Rouna Valley, our attention was caught by a *Scutigera* centipede sitting on a near-by leaf. I had come across a *Scutigera* once before when I was exploring the deep limestone caves outside Port Moresby, but this one was probably a different species. All *Scutigera*, however, survive best in habitats of high humidity and where the light is dim. An unusual feature of this particular centipede is that its front and hind legs are used as antennae.

As darkness gathered, we fol-

AN ALERT GROUND FROG

LAND SNAILS ABOUT TO MATE

OLD MAN'S BEARD LICHEN

lowed a trail into the forest, using our torches to pick out any of the night creatures that would now be active. Wishing to cover as much ground as possible, we decided to split up, arranging a rendezvous where we could meet later to compare animal sightings.

Some kinds of animals were seen by both of us. For instance, one species of ground frog, *Rana daemeli*, was common on both tracks, although we were unable to get close to it. Four inches long, the frogs made astonishing nine-foot leaps out of range, and no amount of stealth brought me any closer. While I was still some yards off, the frogs would jump away and disappear. I glimpsed a giant ground frog, *Rana arfaki*, but this six-inch amphibian also leapt away at my approach.

Both of us saw many land snails. I even came across two of them courting. Snails are hermaphrodite, combining male and female copula-

tory organs in a whitish, pea-shaped protuberance behind the head. As I watched, the courting couple manoeuvred themselves into position for mating. But I did not wait for the happy union to take place as this could have lasted up to five hours.

Flitting fireflies

Walking back to my rendezvous with Eric, I turned off the torch so that I could appreciate the enchantingly soft, green glow of some luminous fungi and the pinpoints of light made by flitting fireflies.

Switching on the torch again, I noticed that almost every third tree I passed was festooned with delicate, pale green old man's beard lichen, *Usnea*. Preferring mist and cool, damp breezes, this plant is also common in the mist forests at altitudes ranging from 8,000 to 11,000 feet.

Shining the torch ahead of me, I saw the silvery glint reflected by the eyes of many spiders. One, a female wolf spider carrying its large, bluish-white egg sac beneath its

abdomen, stopped dead in the beam of light and then scuttled off into the dark undergrowth.

When I met Eric, he told me he had caught a glimpse of a striped possum, *Dactylopsila trivirgata*, which had hastily disappeared among the forest litter. He was particularly delighted to have got a close-up photograph of a large-tailed nightjar, *Caprimulgus macrurus*, as it

A LARGE-TAILED NIGHTJAR

RAIN FOREST AND OWEN STANLEY FOOTHILLS

foothills of the Owen Stanley Range pushing up from the dense rain forest canopy. We passed numerous trees whose trunks were entwined with a species of clematis, a climber that is related to traveller's joy found in England. Some of the shoots were very young, although they would, in time, give forth white or cream flowers.

Leaving the Varirata Park behind, we crossed the strongly undulating Sogeri Plateau. Dipping south-east for about 30 miles, it finally descends in a multitude of interlacing ridges to the Kemp Welch river.

Pushing northwards, we passed through country that had been cultivated for rubber plantations and cattle grazing. There were, however, still substantial tracts of natural

rested in the middle of his path. The nightjar is nocturnal, flying swiftly through the trees to catch insects on the wing. At rest, it sits motionless on the ground, its variegated plumage of browns, blacks, buffs and greys making it almost invisible.

As we were settling down for the night, we heard the loud, repeated call of a nightjar and, picking it out in the beams of our torches, we watched it land near by, apparently oblivious to our presence. It is, in fact, their mottled camouflage that gives nightjars their sense of immunity from danger.

The next morning we set off early under a clear, bright sky on the last eight miles to Ower's Corner and the start of the Kokoda Trail. The forest resounded with bird calls and we

heard the dominant notes of the red-plumed, or Count Raggi's, bird of paradise and the friar bird, *Philomen novaeguineae.*

After a while we saw a friar bird —which was rather a disappointment after hearing its strong and varied calls. About 12 inches long, it is one of the largest honeyeaters; it is also one of the drabbest. The sides of its head are black-skinned and its thin neck and body are covered with short, pale brown feathers.

We walked on through semi-deciduous monsoon forest. Along our path, myriads of spiders' webs hung over and between shrubs and grasses, and where the rays of sunlight struck them, they sparkled with the morning dew. At a break in the forest we saw, away inland, the

SHOOTS OF CLIMBING CLEMATIS

SEEDLING ANT-PLANT ADHERING TO A TRUNK

forest. The trees, which were predominantly evergreen, rose to an average height of 50 feet. There were also deciduous trees, many of which were already losing their leaves. One of these, the okari tree, *Terminalia kaernbachii*, has dark green leaves and bears large, red, lemon-shaped fruits containing the edible okari seeds.

As we moved farther inland, the deciduous trees became more scattered. Small skink lizards dashed for cover in the grass at our approach, creeping out to bask in a spot of sunlight after we had passed.

Bulbous blisters

Among the most curious plants we came across were the epiphytic ant-plants, *Hydnophytum*. Varying in size, they clung to tree trunks and branches like bulbous blisters sprouting a few leaves. Some were mere seedlings only just beginning to develop their bulbous bases; others grew up to two feet in length and from eight to ten inches in diameter. The bases were honeycombed with galleries that had become inhabited by ants, beetles and occasionally even small bats.

Although the ant-plant does not form a true symbiotic relationship with its guests, the ant waste does provide it with nitrogenous material. The life cycles of some ants also appear to be geared to the ant-plant, and studies are being carried out at the University of Papua New Guinea to determine what species of ants shelter in these plants and whether or not each plant species hosts its own species of ant.

We continued across the plateau until reaching the cleared patch of old garden land known as Ower's Corner. Named after a Captain N. Owers who attempted to survey a road from this spot to supply soldiers fighting the Japanese on the Kokoda Trail in 1942, Ower's Corner overlooks the Goldie river flowing 1,200 feet below. On the other side lies the Uberi Bluff, its steep, forest-clad slopes leading down to the village of Uberi, and beyond are the series of ridges rising to the Owen Stanley Range.

Imita, the closest ridge to us, marks the point at which the Japanese advance on Port Moresby was halted and turned back. It was this ridge that we intended to make the final destination on our route. For

BRONZE TECTARIA FERN

BERRIES OF THE RUBIACEAE FAMILY

the first couple of hundred feet of our descent to the Goldie river we passed through grassland that had replaced the original forest. But soon we entered the cool shade of the forest. We knew that from here it stretched almost unbroken across the Owen Stanley Range, and well beyond the town of Kokoda.

Vivid colour

Acorns from the *Lithocarpus* oaks, a feature of the lower and mid-mountain forests, carpeted the ground and were strewn over the trail itself. As we neared the river, short grasses were replaced by mosses, and the forest became dense with vines, palms, thin saplings and large trees. The bright red berries of what was probably a wild member of the coffee family, Rubiaceae, lent

a spot of vivid colour to the prevailing greenness.

There was a variety of ferns interspersed with palms, gingers and other plants. At the mossy base of one tree grew a young *Tectaria* fern. Its shining bronze colour reflected what little light penetrated the forest canopy, giving the fern an illusory thickness.

Eventually we reached the foaming Goldie river at the bottom of the steep slope. The waters, in a mad rush to join those of the Laloki river ten miles farther downstream, swirled round a jumble of gigantic boulders that were jammed against one another. To make our way across the river we had to jump from rock to rock and then finally clamber over some fallen timber that had been brought down by the racing current.

Before picking up the Kokoda Trail on the other side, we rested for a while and noticed the orange, black and white colours of a female ichneumon wasp probing a tree trunk with its long ovipositor in search of a beetle larva. The ovipositor is a hollow tube through which the wasp egg passes inside the wood and into the beetle larva. The wasp egg hatches out and the wasp larva feeds on its host until it emerges as an adult.

Setting off on the Kokoda Trail again, we skirted the Uberi Bluff, choosing the easiest route to Uberi village. On the way, Eric found a spent cartridge embedded in the trail—a reminder of the war. Along the trail we also found heliconias in

bloom. Related to the banana family, their flowers are large and striking, on a stalk often reaching six feet in height. In common with many tropical and sub-tropical plants, the flowering season is not clearly defined and is usually quite prolonged.

Travellers' rest

Uberi village is one of the westernmost villages of the Koiari people and is no more than a collection of half a dozen thatched houses surrounded by gardens. It is used by travellers on the Kokoda Trail as a resting place after the arduous descent from Ower's Corner.

We passed through the village and on to the trail beyond, plodding through luxuriant regrowth on cleared land and carefully avoiding several nettle-like plants, the furry-

HELICONIA IN FLOWER

leaved *Laportea*. These plants can give a nasty sting, but I have seen a native mother brushing her child with a bunch of their leaves in an attempt to counteract stomach ache. Carriers also occasionally beat themselves with the leaves in the hope of staving off fatigue.

After about a quarter of a mile, we entered a tall and magnificent rain forest. There was little undergrowth, but the ground was covered with a thick mat of leaf mould which contrasted with the more open forest where the ground rocks were covered with mosses, ferns and orchids. This undoubtedly was the original, unaltered forest.

Only limited sunlight penetrated the canopy of tree crowns more than a hundred feet above us and it took

AN ICHNEUMON WASP PROBING FOR LARVAE

MALABAR RHODODENDRON

some time for our eyes to become accustomed to the gloom. Small forest birds—flycatchers, fantails and thrushes—moved about in the dim light, but apart from the occasional cry of a cockatoo and the low, persistent humming of insects, the forest was silent. It was also damp: rocks, ground, trees and even the leaves of plants were wet to the touch. Anxious now to reach the end of our journey we walked at a rapid pace, disturbing a lizard that had been busily foraging for insects in the leaf litter.

Imita Ridge was only a short way off when we glanced up through a break in the trees and saw the grey, fast-moving clouds that herald rain. Climbing in this terrain is not easy at the best of times and in a rainstorm it can be positively perilous. Reluctantly, therefore, we decided to abandon our trip to the crest of the ridge and turned back towards Uberi.

Light rain began to fall as we re-entered the village and, although it soon stopped, we took it as fair warning to complete the climb to Ower's Corner as quickly as possible. Just below the crest we passed some Malabar rhododendrons, *Melastoma malabathricum.* This small shrub which, surprisingly, is not at all related to the rhododendron family, is found from the Malabar coast of India right through to Australia. Its clusters of spectacular purple flowers with curved, yellow stamens are followed by berry-like fruits.

When we reached the top of Ower's Corner, clutching our camera equipment for dear life and trying not to slide about on the wet ground, we were still in sunlight, but the ominous rain clouds were gathering fast. Opposite us, Uberi Bluff was black with lichens since the sun never reaches its face, and now the clouds were creeping over it. Turning towards Port Moresby, we felt the first heavy drops of rain falling on our backs.

Perpetual twilight

On our walk we had seen a variety of habitats, including open savannah forest, mixed savannah and monsoon forest, and dense semideciduous forest, and we had ended our walk in primary rain forest, a place of perpetual twilight.

The wild creatures that we had seen were mostly small but were just as fascinating to observe and photograph as larger animals. And in spite of our disappointment at being forced to abandon the climb to the Imita Bluff, we felt more than satisfied with our trip.

LUSH RAIN FOREST BENEATH THE UBERI BLUFF

4/ Through the Rain Forest

*The trees on either side were of enormous size and height,
and their branches were so closely matted together with
parasitical plants, that the sun's rays were excluded, and
we appeared to be walking through a dimly lighted tunnel.*

CAPT. J. A. LAWSON/ *WANDERING IN THE INTERIOR OF NEW GUINEA*

The fringes of the lowland rain forests of Papua New Guinea might
appear, at first sight, to be impenetrable. In between the trees, some
of them draped with D'Albertis' creeper and its brilliant scarlet
flowers, are tangles of lawyer vine, interspersed with shrubs and
lianas that form part of a thick undergrowth. The lawyer vine, widely
known as rattan, is a member of the Calamus group of climbing palms.
It has vicious barbs on long whippy fronds which can trap you. Once
you are hooked in the vine you have no alternative but to back-track,
methodically unhooking yourself on the way.

But, in fact, entering the rain forest is no great problem for there are
numerous trails to follow through breaks in the vegetation. Inside the
forest you can turn your attention to the plants and animals. Small
insects, snakes and lizards forage in the leaf litter underfoot. Flycatchers, honeyeaters, fantails, mouse babblers, cuckoo shrikes, thrushes
and other birds flit in ones and twos among the branches. Where
shafts of sunlight break through the canopy high above, saplings reach
up towards the light; they have grown from some of the millions of
seedlings that lie semi-dormant on the dark forest floor, waiting for
one of the forest giants to fall and leave a gap in the tree canopy.

During the hottest part of the day the forest is almost silent: you can
walk a long way with no sound other than the crackling of twigs under
your feet or the occasional swish and whirr of beating wings as an

alarmed bird flies off to safety. But in the early mornings and evenings there is a constant chatter of small birds and a background buzz of crickets and cicadas; parrots keep up a raucous screeching and birds of paradise call endlessly to one another. Among all these, it is the strong, full-throated voice of the red-plumed bird of paradise that epitomizes for me the spirit of New Guinea.

Tropical rain forest like this is a feature of the lowlands. Its rolling green canopy covers vast tracts of the country, stretching across the river plains, over the fans and terraces, up and down the lowland hills and along the lower slopes of the mountains. There are small areas of dry evergreen forest, mainly acacia and tristania trees, around the Gulf of Papua, and semi-deciduous monsoon forests in the Fly river delta and in other smaller areas, but these are exceptions.

At least 500 different species of trees flourish in the lowland rain forest. The top canopy, from 110 to 150 feet high, is formed by trees buttressed with flanged roots that resemble blades on a huge propeller shaft. Under this top level, there is a variety of lower vegetation, which some botanists divide into four tiers: a sub-canopy of trees about 80 feet high, another layer of smaller trees between 35 and 50 feet high, shrubs under 20 feet and a distinct ground layer of wild aroids, gingers, tree seedlings, mosses, ferns and forest herbs. Crossing the lower tiers and reaching to the crowns of the tallest trees are many climbing plants, creepers, looping lianas, bamboos and rattans.

It is wonderful country to explore, particularly in the remoter regions where the forest remains untouched by the 20th Century. In some areas forest tribes still practise cannibalism. There were certainly cannibals in the Nomad river area of the Great Papuan Plateau when I visited it a few years ago, although in the villages where I stayed I found the people hospitable and friendly. They lived in communal houses about 250 feet long and 60 feet wide, built with a hardwood frame lashed together by "bush rope" made of vines and split rattan. The walls and inside partitions consisted of interlaced split bamboo, laths of black palm, or the midrib of sago leaves, and the roof was thatched with layers of sago palm leaves.

In one village I was invited inside the communal house to look around. The interior was divided into separate areas for communal cooking, eating, talking, working and singing. There were also separate areas for the men's and women's sleeping quarters. At the back of the house was a special room for the initiated men, adorned with row upon row of skulls and the jaw bones of tree kangaroos, cuscuses, ring-tailed possums and bandicoots, as well as the breastbones and plumes of many different birds; I reflected that in some villages the display would have included human skulls and bones as well.

All round the outside walls there were narrow ports for shooting arrows; inside a good stock of weapons, food and water was on hand. The people of the Nomad river live in constant fear of raids by neighbouring villagers and so all the communal houses are well fortified and prepared for a siege. But my main impression was of how neat and tidy everything was; the house was cleaner and certainly better constructed than any of those closer to the government patrol post some 20 miles away, where traditional customs are declining.

On the night I was visiting this village, I went for a walk through the forest to look for nocturnal wildlife. I had to go alone because the people are afraid of evil spirits which are believed to lurk in the forest at night, and so never venture out after dark. It was primary forest with very little undergrowth, for the dense leafy canopy high overhead shaded the lower tiers from the sun and discouraged the spread of undergrowth. Except for the beam from my torch, it was pitch dark with not the faintest glimmer of starlight showing through the trees. There was continuous chirring from the crickets, and somewhere in the distance the doleful, two-note call of a boobook owl, but otherwise very little wildlife was evident. Clearly I was still too close to the village, so I followed a track leading deeper into the bush.

Soon I was attracted by a rustle in the leaves overhead and some growling noises. I shone my torch up and saw two furry, brown ringtailed possums facing each other with bared teeth. As soon as the light caught them, they ceased hostilities and looked down calmly at me, their white stomachs gleaming in the torch beam and their eyes glowing red. This red colour is caused by the tapetum, a reflective layer behind the retina which increases visual efficiency in dim light. For a moment they did not move, then, sensing danger, they ran off in different directions along the branches, quickly disappearing among the leaves.

Farther along I heard the sneeze-like grunting of a bandicoot scratching away in the leaf-mould for worms, beetles, other insects and their larvae. The bandicoot is a marsupial about the size of a big rat, or often much larger, with coarse brown hair, a long, pointed snout and little ears. This one, a male, had a ridiculously short tail. He was quite absorbed in his hunting and took no notice of me standing only a few yards away. For a while I watched him digging under the leaf litter. When he found a big insect, he crushed it with his front paws before

The tubular pink blossoms and long delicate stamens of a shrub in the Acanthaceae family emerge in closely bunched clusters from their club-shaped bracts. Around the branches creep thin, twining vine stems, typical of the abundant secondary plant growth in New Guinea's lowland rain forests.

eating it. As I moved on, he took fright and, with a small raspberry sound of alarm, dashed away.

Flashing my torch around, I noticed a giant rain forest tree whose trunk rose smooth and straight for some 90 feet above the buttress roots, except for one patch marked by what looked like a huge blister. I recognized this as a communal pupal nest of one of the forest moths. Like the processionary caterpillars of other countries, those of Papua New Guinea follow one another from tree to tree. After stripping the leaves, they move on to the next tree. When they are about to pupate, they mass together on the trunk, and the colony—usually about a hundred caterpillars—constructs an enveloping dome of brown silk, inside which each member spins its own silken cocoon. When the time comes for hatching, the moths emerge first from their own cocoons and then from the communal tent. They rest until their wings are dry and strong, and then fly off to mate or find nectar in the forest flowers.

Near a small, quietly flowing stream I came upon a huge olive python. It was at least 15 feet long, and must have shed its skin recently for its reflected rainbow colours glistened in the light of my torch. Slowly and deliberately it slipped through the water across to the opposite bank. The olive python eats other snakes and also mammals and one this size could easily squeeze and suffocate a pig or a wallaby. But they are non-poisonous snakes and, if unprovoked, have a placid temperament, so I followed this one across the stream to have a closer look. As I got near, it raised its head up to my waist to see what I was and its long, forked tongue poked out to touch my hand. It retreated a little, then came back and touched my hand again. Apparently I did not pass muster as a potential meal, because the python lowered its head to the ground and started to crawl away. I tried to pick it up but it was too long and heavy.

Suddenly I heard a kingfisher close at hand. Kingfishers are usually considered to be diurnal birds, flying about and feeding during the day; but there are a couple of species that are active by night, and one of these, the hook-billed kingfisher, is common in the lowland rain forests throughout Papua New Guinea. Their call is a rather mournful ascending trill of three or four notes. I soon located this kingfisher, but when I shone the torch on it, the bird stopped calling and stared inquisitively back at me. It was about the size of a cricket ball and nearly as round, with a short, stiff tail, flat crowned head and large bill. Its body was mostly chestnut brown with spots of yellow ochre, except for a cap of cornflower blue mixed with brown and yellow.

Two types of palm—the slender, solitary Metroxylon and the tightly bunched Gulubia—mingle with giant trees up to 150 feet high to form a dense canopy of lowland rain forest. Beneath the leafy roof there are several further tiers of trees and a layer of shrubs. Tree seedlings, ferns and mosses grow where limited sunlight filters through to the forest floor.

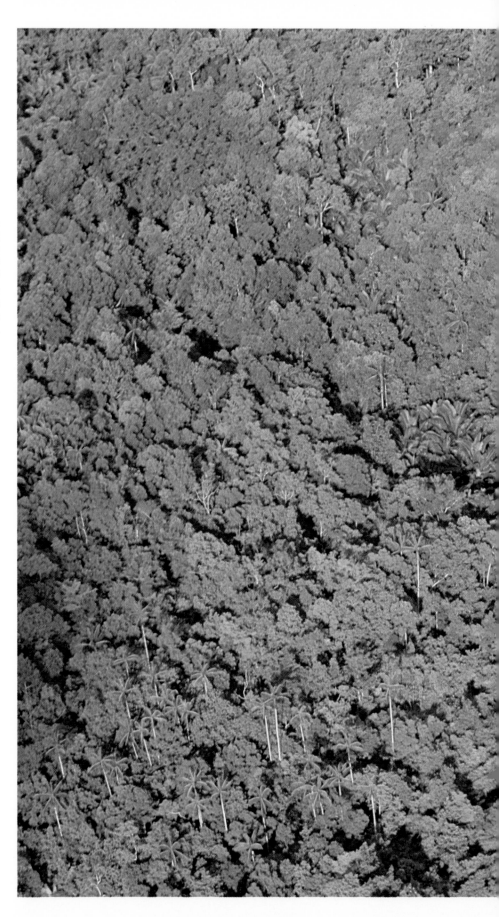

A silvery reflection of something on the ground caught my attention as I walked slowly back to the village. It was the shiny track of slime made by a land planarian, or flatworm, as it crawled along. The planarian has a pointed head which seems to merge into its body so that it is hardly distinguishable as a head, but is more like a probe. This planarian, four inches long, was black and brown with a line of small black and yellow-brown lozenges down the centre of its back. These worms are always found in moist places and they quickly shrivel and die in dry environments.

Near by I found a giant millepede foraging in the leaf mould beside a fallen log. I switched off my torch, and its cigar-shaped body glowed faintly luminous in the darkness. The luminosity is thought to be a warning signal to predators rather than a recognition sign for other millepedes. Unlike centipedes, which have one pair of legs on each body segment, millepedes have two pairs on most of their segments and the number of segments is variable. This particular specimen was about eight inches long, and when I turned it over it curled up for a moment before writhing over on to its legs and crawling off. Millepedes are vegetarians; for defence they can eject an acrid liquid that stains the hands and causes intense skin-burning, and is an effective deterrent against attacks by birds and small animals.

Back at the longhouse all was quiet. I crawled into my sleeping bag and lay awake for what seemed like a very long time listening to the night life of the forest—the unceasing chorus of crickets and in the distance the call of the kingfisher.

Next day I was due to accompany an army patrol through the forest to another village some six miles away. Soldiers of the Papua New Guinea army participate in patrols through different types of country to augment the work of the government, and are stationed at various points in the interior, bringing the remoter tribes into contact with more sophisticated ways of life and introducing them by easy stages to systems of law, justice, education and health care.

We set off shortly after dawn. In the main, it was easy walking country: a slightly undulating plateau with an open forest floor between the trees. But there were a number of small streams to cross, and they were a constant worry to me because they were usually bridged only by a single slippery log. Rather shamefacedly I avoided crossing the first stream by log, preferring instead to clamber down the bank, slosh through the shallow water and climb up the other side. But when we got to the next one, I saw a medium-sized crocodile lurking under an

A six-inch long giant millepede works its way along a mossy tree trunk. An inoffensive creature, the millepede curls up when disturbed, relying on its hard outer coat for protection. If provoked it will secrete a noxious fluid from a row of glands down each side of its body.

overhang on the river bank upstream and quickly forgot my mistrust of the slippery-looking logs.

Leaf litter, in places four inches thick, covers the ground in the rain forest and collects in drifts between the buttress roots of the trees. Always damp and warm, it provides both a home and a food supply for countless creatures. As we made our way along the track, lizards were running about everywhere. Creepers, vines, orchids, ferns and lianas festooned the trees, some of which were doomed giants dying in the ever-tightening embrace of the strangler fig. Where trees had fallen, a circle of sunlight highlighted the rich colours of the leaves.

At the edge of one small clearing I saw a large goura pigeon sitting on a branch fairly high up in the trees. Its deep-throated booming call was taken up by another bird deeper in the forest. The goura is the biggest pigeon in the world, growing to about 30 inches in height, and its flesh is regarded as a delicacy by the natives.

As we walked on I heard the swishing noise made by the powerful wings of a hornbill disturbed by our approach. It is a distinctive sound, rather like the puffing of a steam locomotive. Hornbills used to be common birds of the rain forest, and although they are fewer now, you often hear them in the early mornings when they fly from their roosts to feeding areas. At dusk you can see their silhouettes strung out in lines against the reddening sky as they return.

Cassowaries, giant flightless birds related to emus, are also common in the Nomad river area because the human population is sparse and bows and arrows are still the normal hunting weapons. I caught glimpses of several before the "shootboy" accompanying our patrol shot and killed one. Pigeons and cassowaries are welcome supplements to the usual patrol diet of rice and tinned meat. This was a common or double-wattled cassowary, best known of the three species found in Papua New Guinea. It stood about four feet six inches to the shoulder; it had a shaggy coat of thin, black feathers hiding the rudimentary remains of its wings; there was a horny black casque on its head, and its neck, bare of feathers, glowed with patches of blue, red and yellow.

The cassowary is the only flightless bird (apart from the New Zealand kiwi) that lives in the forest in preference to savannahs and plains. It is a clumsy creature and its progress is often marked by the sound of snapping branches. But it can run at speeds of up to 30 miles an hour and jump high obstacles with a single bound. In many parts of Papua New Guinea, cassowary chicks are traded between tribes and bred for food. Adult birds are always kept in pens, for the cassowary's

An oceanic gecko, its vertical pupils contracting in the photographer's flash, leaps from branch to branch in its nocturnal search for insects. Besides its sharp claws, this lizard also has tiny, hooklike clinging devices under each toe, enabling it to gain a grip on the most precarious surfaces.

powerful foot is armed with a long, sharp claw on the inner of its three toes, and one slash of it can kill.

Almost anywhere you walk in the lowland rain forest of Papua New Guinea in the morning or the evening, you are likely to see a variety of screeching parrots. This morning was no exception. In the space of less than an hour I saw a pair of eclectus parrots nesting in the hollow of a tall, dead tree, as well as the extraordinary long-beaked vulturine parrot, a giant, black palm cockatoo, many red-cheeked parrots and several flocks of 20 to 30 rainbow lorikeets; the glittering red, green, blue and yellow hues of the lorikeets made a splash of colour against the green of the forest canopy. There are more than 40 different species of parrots in the country, including the smallest in the world, the diminutive pygmy parrot, which is no more than three inches long and nests in tunnels burrowed into tree termite nests.

The magnificent bird of paradise tends to be heard more often than seen. A sudden flash of red, yellow, green and purple plumage, a brief glimpse of outspread wings or trailing, wire-like tail plumes in the high foliage is often all you see to mark the passage of a splendidly garbed individual. The elaborate nuptial displays that take place in the tree-tops are seldom observed, but some species flaunt themselves more openly during the mating and nesting season and the displays may continue on and off throughout the day.

We were about half way to our village when I heard several red-plumed birds of paradise calling from a point a short way off the track. Hoping there might be a display tree near by, I went on ahead of the patrol, slipping quietly through the forest in the direction of the calls. I was delighted when I found a tree with five male birds in it, all in full throat. Each bird had staked its claim to one or two branches as private display territory and was spreading and depressing its wings to expose the rich red feathers of the flanks in two shimmering fountains of colour. While calling he would dip his head between his depressed wings and, in a paroxysm of ecstasy, vibrate his body, wings and plumes to give a scintillating display of fine feathers.

There must have been 15 females flitting about in the trees near by. I could see that it would be hard for a female to make up her mind with so many magnificent and ardent wooers to choose from. Occasionally, one would come on to the branch of a male, who would then call and dance with increased vigour, at the same time performing little hops, along the branch, gradually shortening the distance between himself and his intended mate. At the last moment she would crouch in sub-

An adult female dwarf cassowary, about three and a half feet tall, paces through the New Guinea rain forest. Although quite common in the rain forest, these flightless birds are very shy. Often the only signs of their presence are the distinctive tracks made by their sharp claws, and droppings filled with stones from the fruits they swallow whole.

mission or dash off in a flurry of shyness—although not too far away. Provided she did not lose her place to another, more forward female in the meantime, she would soon be back to tempt him again. Once mating had occurred, the male would lose interest in his partner and eventually look out for another.

I stayed so long watching this scene that it was some time before I was able to catch up with the patrol. They were just leaving the primary forest about a mile from the village and were passing through some secondary growth and old village garden land. I had been warned before I came to the Nomad river that the place crawled with leeches, but I had seen only a few—until now. The ground and the plants were alive with them. If I stopped on the track for a moment I would see up to a score looping along the path in my direction, while others reached out from the shrubs on either side, waiting for me to brush against them. Being clad in long woolly socks and canvas leggings, I provided ideal conditions for the leeches to carry on their bloodthirsty activities. They were small enough to squirm through eyelets of the leggings or crawl through the socks to fasten themselves to my feet and legs. When we arrived at the village I took off my boots and socks to find my feet swimming in blood. This happened on several occasions in that forest. Luckily, leeches do not seem to transfer any disease, but their bites itch and dangerous sores can result from scratching and infecting these.

I have always counted myself fortunate that I am not very allergic to insect bites. I felt particularly fortunate on the occasion some time later when I was wandering through the rain forest looking for lizards. I found most of them on top of tree trunks and fallen logs; but some were hiding underneath. A slight buzzing sound should have warned me to be careful as I approached one log, for when I lifted it a swarm of small, black wasps dashed at my face. I do not know how I managed to escape with only two or three stings because the horde seemed to envelop me before I could move. I crashed through the forest like a mad bull, felling saplings and snapping vines in my efforts to put at least a mile between me and that nest. The stings were painful but had no lasting effect.

The tiny, pale red-brown bush mites, or mokka, that infest the floor of most lowland forests can be equally unpleasant. Individually these mites are almost invisible, but you are soon made aware of their presence as they climb over exposed skin. They cause intense itching, and are vectors of scrub typhus from rats to man. The rare cases of this disease are effectively treated with chloromycetin, but before and during the

Second World War scrub typhus caused many deaths among the troops.

There is very little hunting of wildlife around the Nomad river and the area is so remote that it is unlikely to suffer much ecological disruption for years to come. In other lowland forest areas of Papua New Guinea the disruption has already begun. Not long after I arrived in Port Moresby I regularly visited a patch of monsoon forest about 30 miles from the town to study some populations of honeyeaters. We would net and band them with numbered aluminium rings, and on subsequent trips we would try to catch the same birds to record changes in plumage and to establish the duration of their residence. This area is now planted with introduced teak. The forest as we knew it is gone. Farther along the road, a magnificent forest of tall jungle trees, which once teemed with wildlife and were draped with orchids and D'Albertis' creeper, is now being cleared to make way for farming.

The demands being made on the land by the introduction of a cash economy require further destruction of the rain forest for cattle grazing, tea, coffee and rubber plantations and monotypic forest plantations. Even worse is the extraction of timber for export from hundreds of acres of original forest without adequate re-afforestation. The rate of exploitation of Papua New Guinea's resources is staggeringly fast.

There is no better example of what is happening than in the West Sepik District, in the north-west of the country. I went there for the first time several years ago with a colleague to investigate reported finds of prehistoric stone club heads, axe blades and other objects. Little is known about the prehistoric stone culture of Papua New Guinea, so any evidence of types and distribution of stone implements is worth following up. We had arranged to stay at a mission station deep in the rain forest, and the quickest way of getting there was by air.

Looking down from a monoplane over mile after mile of unbroken forest, I was comforted to see how unspoiled most of the country still was. Suddenly we plunged down into a narrow valley towards the tiny airstrip. The pilot put us down safely and took off again at once, leaving me and my companion standing on the edge of the airstrip. We were surrounded by a dense wall of tall rain forest trees; there was no doubt that we were in a wilderness. We waited in the shade for native carriers to arrive. Birds seemed to be calling all around us—which was unusual, as it was the hottest time of the day, when they are usually silent. We did not wait long. When our guides arrived they told us we had a five-mile trek to the mission. It turned out to be a delightful walk.

As soon as we entered the forest we became aware of the great wealth of wildlife all about us. White-throated fantails, rufous thrushes and ground thrushes were all calling as we moved along the track. Honeyeaters and flowerpeckers fed on blossoms and small berries. A lowland eupetes, an immaculate bird of cerulean hue with a black stripe through the eye and a snow-white bib, hopped along the ground, neck erect, keeping a weather eye on us.

At one point, we spotted a group of white-shouldered wrens at the side of the track. I whistled to them and they gradually moved closer until a resplendent male, with mat black plumage and white shoulder stripe, ventured to the very edge of the track. Brown females came up too, hopping in and out of the grass, their tails standing erect like little flags. They became nervous when they saw us and soon moved on.

Birds of paradise were calling everywhere. Some of the time entire groups sang in harmony, but occasionally I was able to pick out a pair calling in melodious counterpoint. I decided to make an experiment by imitating their call and soon had the pair answering me. Cautiously they came closer, until they were in the tops of the trees 300 feet away. We continued to answer each other for several minutes before they decided it was a waste of time and flew away. All along the path I found different plants: peperomia creepers, staghorn and bird's nest ferns, gingers, climbing palms, orchids and aroids. Lizards, spiders, centipedes, birdwing butterflies, stick insects, millepedes and snakes were all there. The place was like a well-stocked zoo.

But this exquisite wilderness is now threatened by changes brought about by man. The need for new garden land among the tribes surrounding the forest has caused the fringe areas to be eaten away as old garden soil becomes sterile. An expanding population has accelerated the process and now gardening land is so scarce that there is pressure on the landholders to open up more areas for cultivation.

If any of this rain forest is to survive, it will have to be preserved as a national park. Since change has come to Papua New Guinea, the need for establishing national parks has become accepted. But there is no time to waste. So far as we know, not a single forest animal has become extinct through man's interference in Papua New Guinea. Few other countries can make such a boast. It will be a pity if the record is spoilt.

Animals at Sundown

Dusk falls swiftly in the rain forest of New Guinea. As the shadows deepen and the air begins to cool, the myriad birds and insects of the daytime retreat to their resting places. Suddenly the forest erupts with sound as the crickets, cicadas and other creatures of the dusk emerge from their hiding places and begin to stir and call.

In the fading light, brightly coloured tree frogs creep out from beneath leaves and loose bark, and start to hunt insects; the males in their shrill voices advertising their presence to other frogs. Bats unfurl their wings and leave their roosts, some to hunt down the insects that swarm through the forest at nightfall, while others such as the tube-nosed fruit bat (right), search for fruiting trees. Unlike the insectivorous species, the tube-nosed bat has no echo-location system to help it navigate through the tangled branches, relying instead on its excellent vision.

As darkness deepens, nocturnal mammals, including the arboreal spotted cuscus, also wake to begin their nightly search for food. A woolly-coated marsupial, the spotted cuscus moves slowly through the trees on the lookout for its favourite leaves and fruit, as well as for insects and birds' eggs. It is joined by its close relative, the ground cuscus, which is only partly arboreal and frequently forages for small rodents and insects on the forest floor. It often hides in holes at the base of trees during the day. Although the wide eyes of the cuscus seem to stare vacantly, it has the acute vision characteristic of most nocturnal mammals.

Marsupial "mice", as well as true rodents, prowl through the undergrowth, along hanging vines and in the trees, attracting the attention of the owls, whose senses are finely attuned to hunting in the dark. The owls' retinas contain huge concentrations of rods, the nerve cells that receive light, while large and highly developed ears enable them to pinpoint sounds with great accuracy.

The growing darkness brings out reptiles like the green tree python and brown tree snake, which glide silently along branches in search of frogs and sleeping birds. About 30 minutes after the first fading of the light, the choral cacophony has largely ended and the creatures of the dusk cease activity, leaving those of the night to continue their search for food in the dark forest.

Still wrapped tightly within its wings, this tube-nosed fruit bat has just awakened for the evening and will soon be foraging for its favourite fruits. The nostril pipes, which are up to half an inch long, are directed away from the fruit while the bat takes a bite so that juice does not run into its nose.

A male spotted cuscus (above), one of New Guinea's many marsupials, edges its way down a tree trunk. Active throughout the night, it is well adapted to its arboreal life-style, having a partly bare, prehensile tail and strong, curved claws that enable it to climb trees and cling to branches.

Two ground cuscuses (right) sniff the air for danger. Closely related to the spotted cuscus, these short-haired, omnivorous animals move through a range of habitats, from mangrove swamps, where they catch crabs and mudskippers, to mountain forests, where they eat rodents, berries and flowers.

A sooty owl (above) surveys the forest floor for insects. Its large eyes are far keener than a human's and similarly placed at the front of the head to give binocular vision; but they lack mobility and cannot be rotated. To compensate, the owl is able to swivel its head through an angle of 270 degrees.

A boobook owl (right), having just caught a large insect, splays out its tail and wing feathers as it comes in to land. The wings, which are large in relation to the body, enable it to fly with few wing beats. This characteristic, together with the downy softness of its feathers, makes the owl silent in attack.

A green tree frog (above) is caught in the glare of the photographer's flash. The tips of the fingers and toes are enlarged into disc-like adhesive pads that enable the frog to cling to the undersides of smooth leaves during the day, when it is at rest.

Its vocal sac ballooned with air, a tree frog (right) pipes out its mating call to any females that may be in the vicinity. The elastic sac, which contracts to lie unobtrusively beneath its mouth when not inflated, serves to amplify the sound of the tiny creature's voice.

The green tree python (left) is speckled yellow when young, but by the time it reaches adulthood, it will appear in its regulation green livery. It eats rodents and small birds, suffocating them and drawing them into its gullet with large, curved teeth.

A brown tree snake (right), uncoiling its slender body from a branch, flicks out its forked tongue. When it is tracking down prey, the snake's tongue picks up scent particles from the air and transfers them for analysis to a sensory apparatus called Jacobson's organ, which is located on the roof of the mouth.

An angle-headed agamid drapes itself across some branches as it settles down for the night. The lizard, which has pursued spiders and insects until the last minute of dusk, assumes this position so that nocturnal predators will think it is part of the tree.

5/ Savannah and Swamp

The silence is absolute, the merciless heat intolerable.
As far as the eye can see tall grasses flash, stiff as
steel blades, tinted green and yellow.   ANDRE DUPEYRAT/ *PAPUA*

When I first came to New Guinea and landed at Port Moresby I was surprised and disillusioned. From explorers' tales I had a mental picture of valleys and jagged mountains covered from coast to coast in rain forest, and what I saw was quite the opposite. A drier, drabber landscape, I thought, could be found only in a desert. I could hardly believe it.

Nobody had told me that along the Central Province coast of Papua New Guinea there is an area where little rain falls for eight months of the year. Port Moresby lies in a 100-mile belt of hilly savannah grassland dotted with trees and interrupted at intervals by mangrove swamps or an occasional pocket of rain forest. Later I found that this belt of coastal savannah ends less than 20 miles inland. I discovered, too, that the savannah has a fascination and beauty of its own.

Now I often go exploring around Port Moresby. The savannah wildlife there is noticeably distinct from that of the rain forest; in fact, it bears a closer relationship with the Australian continent. I always make a point of listing the animals I see on my field trips, and the differences emerge clearly. On a journey through the savannah into the rain forest, easy to make in one day, my bird list will show two different groups of species, those of the savannah and those of the forest. I always try to reach the shelter of the forest by noon, when the baking heat of the savannah is at its worst. Imagine pushing through grass which in places reaches far above your head, tickling your ears and getting in your eyes. It is stifling. The breeze that sweeps above the grass cannot reach your body; the trees are few, and for most of the time the sun relentlessly burns down on your head. Even where the grass is short the breeze is hot. So it is a relief to enter the cool gloom of the forest.

Twelve miles north of Port Moresby lie two small mountains, connected to each other by a small saddle and grandiosely named Mount Lawes and Little Mount Lawes. They are mostly covered by savannah woodland, but here and there on their slopes there is semi-deciduous monsoon forest, quite dense and matted in parts. I once took an archaeologist to visit the site of a prehistoric native village on the slopes of Little Mount Lawes. We left our car at the saddle between the two hills and set off on foot through the surrounding savannah.

The dry season was well advanced, and much of the grass had died; some had been burned off by the local people on hunting trips, to frighten wallabies out into the open. The lack of grass made walking relatively easy. The trees were spread out as in an open wood, and we could see through them for about 200 yards. As we walked along, grassland birds such as the blue-winged kookaburra and the honey-eating friar bird flew across our path, and we could hear others calling from the eucalyptus trees. The harsh, grating calls of several fawn-breasted bower birds in a small patch of vine and scrub attracted our attention, and we went over to investigate. I suspected that a bower, the birds' dancing playground, might be there, and I was right: after crawling about in the thicket for a while I found a fine bower under an overhang of branches and leaves.

The archaeologist was intrigued to see the bower. It was built of thin sticks stood on end to form a roofless corridor about twelve inches long, 18 inches high and just wide enough for the bird to hop through. There was a platform of sticks at each end of the bower, and one platform was decorated with bright green berries. Similar berries were draped over the tops of the walls.

I told my companion how the male builds the bower, decorates it, and then waits in it. The females are attracted and gather to watch the male's courtship dance. When he has an audience he comes out and dips his head, showing his neck feathers to the females. This part of the performance is intriguing, since the species of bower birds found in the Port Moresby savannah have quite ordinary neck feathers, much like those of the head and back. Other species in Australia display a collar of bright pink feathers at the nape of the neck. Some scientists argue that the Papuan bower bird has lost its coloured neck feathers

DECORATING THE BOWER

The Bower Bird's Bower

The male fawn-breasted bower bird—found only in savannah areas of eastern New Guinea and northern Australia—is an ardent seducer, spending three days preparing a sturdy bower or wooing chamber. He meshes sticks and twigs into a rectangular platform up to three feet long and 14 inches high on which he erects the actual bower: two short parallel walls of sticks which enclose an intimate mating space. Finally, he decorates both platform and bower with green berries.

His bower complete, the male performs a mating dance on the platform, enticing the female inside. If the subsequent mating is successful, it is she who goes off to build a tree nest in which she rears the young.

THE MALE WINS A MATE

while retaining the gesture that once displayed them; others think that the Papuan species never evolved coloured feathers.

Sometimes the male bower bird carries the green decorative berries in his bill while dancing. When one of the females has been sufficiently impressed, the pair mate at the bower. Studies of one species of bower bird have shown that the male is polygamous, and this probably holds true of other species. After performing each elaborate ritual the male leaves the female to build a nest in a tall tree, sit on the eggs and rear the fledglings on her own.

When he is not dancing, the male bird spends a lot of time fussing about the bower, rearranging the berries on the platform or realigning the sticks in the walls. He also "paints" the walls—an extraordinary act for which there does not seem to be any satisfactory explanation. Watching from hides, I have seen the birds paint with what looked like mud and moss in their bills; on one occasion I saw a bird using a pulped berry. The birds seem to chew the material, mix it with saliva, then rub the resultant pulpy wad on the inside walls of the bower. When the archaeologist and I came upon this bower, the birds had moved away; but I was able to show my companion some fresh, greenish brown paint on the sticks of one bower wall.

We moved on. Cuckoo-shrikes, willy wagtails, lemon-breasted flycatchers, rainbow lorikeets and several other birds typical of the savannah were easy to see or hear. Just as we rounded a large eucalyptus tree, we surprised a grassland creature known as the agile wallaby. This small cousin of the kangaroo is a common animal in the savannah of southern Papua New Guinea, and can be found in the same type of terrain in northern Australia. It is sandy haired with a whitish stripe along the side of its face and stands about three feet high. It was hard to judge who got the biggest surprise, us or the wallaby, for it flashed away from beneath our feet at lightning speed.

We crossed a few low ridges on the slope of Little Mount Lawes, and sighted the wall of the forest ahead of us. The site of the prehistoric village lay on a flat ridge at the edge of the forest. On our way over we disturbed a deer, which fled, and I stumbled over a goat's skull hidden in the grass. Both deer and goats are introduced animals. Reaching our objective, we spent a hot and uncomfortable half hour searching the ground for the remains of cooking fires or bones from animals the people had eaten. A few stone adze blades and many fragments of clay pots lay about, but we left them where they were, only recording them so that a proper survey and a small excavation could be made another

Its stomach distended by a partly digested meal, an amethystine rock python basks on the edge of a forest clearing. Although it is the largest species of snake to be found in New Guinea and may reach a length of 22 feet, its body is usually no thicker than a man's arm. But its skin has sufficient elasticity to allow animals as large as wallabies to be swallowed without difficulty. This snake is non-venomous and kills larger animals by crushing and suffocating them.

time. By now our soaked shirts clung to our backs. We pushed into the forest and found immediate relief in the shade, cooling off before the walk back to our car and the drive home.

The time to explore the savannah by car is after dark, for it is surprising how much wildlife can be picked out by the headlights. One night as I drove with my wife and two sons about 20 miles along the road to the Vaimauri river, we noticed a barn owl sitting on a roadside post. We stopped and got out to have a look at the owl, which seemed not at all concerned by our presence. Then we saw a four-foot carpet python stretched across the road. The owl was plainly interested in the snake, although I doubted whether it would have the courage to attack it. These snakes grow up to 13 feet in Australia, but in Papua New Guinea seldom reach more than six feet. I picked up the python, which was swollen with a recent meal, and let it go in the grass at the roadside.

As we drove on we saw a different owl species, the barking owl. This bird sometimes gives a spine-chilling shriek which has earned it the nickname of "screaming woman bird". I have never heard that sound but know the bird's normal call, a double-noted cry like the distant bark of a dog. We also spotted a very small mouse-like creature which ran across the road. We could not identify it before it vanished into the tall savannah grass, but a rare and tiny marsupial "mouse" known as a planigale is found in the Moresby area, and we wondered if this was one.

Instead of having a pair of chisel-like front teeth typical of a placental rodent, this furry, pouched mammal possesses a series of small teeth—incisors, canines, premolars and molars—like other carnivorous mammals; it is remarkably ferocious for its size, attacking animals considerably larger than itself.

Farther along, we saw a bandicoot trotting along the edge of the grass. He started to cross the road, then hesitated. I turned off the engine, and watched him as he stopped in the glare of the headlights, twitching his ears about like little radar dishes. He seemed to sense that there was no danger, and dashed across the road. My family and I have kept bandicoots in temporary captivity in Australia in order to photograph them, and have found them engaging animals. The female bandicoot has a pouch which opens at the bottom, unlike the female kangaroo whose pouch opens at the top and looks like an apron pocket when she stands upright. The bandicoot, moving close to the ground on all fours, would find sticks and stones a constant menace if her pouch opened at the top. Her young run behind her as she walks and jump between her hind legs into the pouch.

We disturbed several nightjars during our drive. There are about 67 species of this bird distributed through the warmer regions of the world, and Papua New Guinea has six of them, found both in savannah and forest. The ones we saw were the commonest species, the large-tailed nightjar. During the day they rest on the forest floor among the leaves, protected by their camouflage. At night they hawk about chasing insects, their fluttering flight making them look like giant moths. They often rest on the roads at night where they become dazzled by car headlights and are fairly easy to catch. As we were leaving, we moved one nightjar out of danger only to see it flutter a short distance and land on the road again.

The Port Moresby coastal strip of savannah has one of the lowest rainfalls in Papua New Guinea, and three months after the wet season the small creeks are dry. Late in the dry season reptiles are encountered more often than usual. I have frequently walked through this savannah country when all the grass is dead or burnt off, and I have found legless lizards, black whip snakes and taipan snakes on the move, looking either for water or for animals that have moved closer to water.

Recently my family and I disturbed a very large taipan snake. We were walking along the escarpment of the Astrolabe Range behind Port Moresby, following a path that runs through heathland and short grass. Snakes are usually just as frightened of humans as we are of them. But in this case we had the more cause to be alarmed. The taipan is one of the deadliest snakes in the world: an average specimen about six feet long carries enough venom to kill more than a hundred people. Moreover the taipan is strong, vigorous and fast moving, so it is one of the most difficult snakes to handle. Having disturbed this individual, I knew that the most sensible course of action would be to let him slip away through the undergrowth. But I dearly wanted to get some photographs of a taipan. After some skirmishing in the grass, I managed to catch him by the tail and lift him off the ground. This annoyed him excessively and he twisted this way and that in an attempt to bite my hand or some other part of my anatomy. It took quite a bit of juggling to pop him into the sack I had with me.

This was just to quieten him down. When I found a patch of open ground where he could not disappear too quickly, I slid him gently out of the bag. Immediately he slithered underneath it. After setting up my camera and arming my wife, Margaret, with a long stick, we prepared for action. Margaret lifted the bag off the snake with the stick. He raised his head a little, and I took a shot from just one yard away. Slowly and smoothly I wound the crank of the camera for another picture, praying that the movement would not send him racing away. He stood his ground, flicking his tongue in and out. A few more shots, a slow step back, and then we watched his glistening, rich chestnut brown form glide swiftly over the sandy soil and vanish into the grass. We would have enjoyed watching him a little longer, but there was a noticeable lessening of tension when he had gone.

The Port Moresby strip is the driest stretch of savannah in Papua New Guinea, but not the largest. In the far south-west corner of the mainland there is a great expanse of low-lying land known as the Bensbach Plains. Together, the Bensbach Plains and the Port Moresby strip account for almost the whole of Papua New Guinea's savannah. Situated just north of the Torres Strait, these zones provide a reminder of the physical link that once existed between the Australian continent and New Guinea. Until the land bridge across the strait was gradually submerged about 40,000 years ago this part of New Guinea was joined with northern Queensland, and the New Guinea savannah still maintains close affinities with the savannah woodland of the Australian area, both in vegetation and wildlife.

The Bensbach Plains consist of savannah, woodland with eucalyptus, and marshland covering thousands of acres between the Torres Strait

A taipan, one of the deadliest snakes in the world, coils its six-foot length into a defensive stance before gliding swiftly away. Belonging to the same group as coral snakes and cobras, the taipan is more lethal than either.

and the Fly river. From August to November they are bare, baking and parched. You can walk for mile after mile across open grassland dotted with a few isolated trees. A line of foliage on the horizon tells of a distant river or lagoon; otherwise the landscape is featureless. But for the remaining eight months of the year the plains are inundated with floodwaters that spread from the Fly river across to the Merauke river in Irian Jaya, and the entire area is transformed into a giant swamp.

The Bensbach Plains attract a wide range of wildlife at all times of the year, but the animals are most in evidence at the beginning and end of the wet season. Herds of deer and wallabies roam freely across the vast expanses of short, lush grass, pausing occasionally to drink from the many scattered pools. There are a thousand daily encounters. Groups of angry, squawking birds wheel and swoop down on the carcass of a deer. Huge crows fight for their share of the meat and are chased away by the whistling kites. A large sand goanna, or monitor lizard, rears up on its hind legs, angrily puffs out his throat, and does his best to frighten off the other scavengers.

One reason for the large animal population of the Bensbach Plains is that the annual flooding makes the area virtually uninhabitable by man. The animals, being unused to humans, are remarkably tame. I have come across a pair of agile wallabies who simply stopped and stared, twitching their ears and scratching their stomachs with their forepaws; then, deciding I was harmless, hopped slowly away to continue feeding. Deer are excessively hunted in the Port Moresby savannah, but here they thrive. The dominant species is the rusa, introduced into Dutch New Guinea (now Irian Jaya) from Indonesia in 1913. They have spread into Papua, and now there are up to 70,000 on the Bensbach Plains. They, too, are quite approachable. When grazing, only a few will casually raise their heads to make sure nobody comes too close. They are alert to other animal predators, though. Once I was idly watching a herd of about 50 rusa deer when I heard barking in the distance. The entire herd instantly raced away. Moments later a lone deer sped past, chased by a snapping, snarling pack of feral dogs.

The change from dry to wet seasons on the Bensbach Plains can come very suddenly, with torrential rains. This is vividly illustrated by the experiences of two army patrols that visited the plains a few months apart. The first patrol, out on a training course in September, had to ration its water supply drastically. The clay of the plains was rock-hard and so dry that even when the soldiers managed to sink wells in depressions they failed to find any water. The second patrol in early

December found the same area inundated. These soldiers continuously splashed through swamp water that reached to their knees. At night they had to sleep on platforms of sticks built in the branches of trees. Once, as nightfall approached, they headed for a small island of dry ground, but found it was already occupied by snakes and other animals. Hastily they reverted to their perches in the trees.

When the floodwaters recede, lagoons and tracts of swamp remain, providing a rich habitat for all forms of wildlife, especially birds. The average person tends to think of marshes and swamps as foul places, and looks askance at the naturalist who, covered in mud and mosquitoes, spends many hours prying into the lives of the animals. I am one of those who are happy watching the wildlife in these uncomfortable but fascinating haunts. Birds assemble in such numbers on the black, gluey mudbanks of the rivers or around the lagoons that when they rise and fly away en masse they almost blot out the sun. The eye-catching magpie geese, with their unusually long black necks and pink legs, often prefer to perch high in the trees. From their vantage point they survey the crowded scene below: thousands of ducks jostling one another, and black-necked storks strutting around as if they were policing the movements of the bird multitude.

Brolgas, beautiful soft-grey cranes related to the sarus cranes of Asia, mingle with the throng. As with other members of the crane family, their mating ceremonies are spectacular. The male and the female dance round each other, stretching, bowing, and every so often leaping high in the air in a dance of exuberant sensuality. I have seen hundreds of them cavorting together; and their antics are not necessarily confined to the mating season.

Several Australian birds are also found here, and nowhere else in Papua. Such visitors include the black-backed magpie, the black-faced wood-swallow, the wedge-tailed eagle and the Australian bustard. Large flocks of migratory birds often come down to roost on the Bensbach Plains and on the edges of the marshes and lagoons. Sharp-tailed sandpipers, little stints, little whimbrels, and Mongolian dotterels feed together in the tussocks of grass on the banks and at the water's brim. Groups of royal spoonbills slowly advance through the shallows, heads swaying in an arc from side to side as they sift the muddy water with their flattened beaks. Marsh terns and brahminy kites swoop over the surface of the water, while white-bellied sea eagles glide high overhead.

These sea eagles are majestic birds of prey, and their antics during the mating season are astonishing. I once watched a pair of them because it

Its white plumage elegantly silhouetted against the dark blue water, a royal or black-billed spoonbill wades through a pool in the Bensbach Plains of southern Papua. Moving gracefully through the shallows, the spoonbill swings its partly open beak from side to side in the water, seeking the tiny aquatic animals on which it feeds.

seemed they were fighting, but I soon realized that they were indulging in an elaborate courtship display. One eagle skimmed along in a straight line while the second bird swooped up from below, turned upside down and presented a small branch to its mate. Sometimes when parting with the branch—or receiving it back—the lower bird would perform a complete roll; twice it veered off in an almost vertical dive, plummeting down at breakneck speed and then suddenly pulling up to climb swiftly again and rejoin its partner. Considering the large size of the birds, the speed and grace of their movements were amazing. I have also watched these eagles fishing, and can vouch for their skill. On the lagoons of the Bensbach Plains they will glide smoothly down to snatch fish from the surface of the water with hardly a pause in their flight.

The swamplands of Papua New Guinea include areas that are permanently awash. Huge expanses of river delta, half land and half water, provide the lowlands with a mushy fringe of mudbanks and swamp forest. These are among the largest swamplands in the tropical world, fed in the north by the Sepik and Ramu rivers and in the south by the Fly and Purari. The northern basin, carrying the Sepik and Ramu rivers, is an area of New Guinea that is subsiding, allowing water gradually to rise and invade the surrounding river valleys, and the swamplands extend from the sea to the foot of the mountains.

I think this must be the hottest and most unpleasant place in Papua New Guinea. When you are out in a motor canoe with no overhead protection, the sun scorches your face. The air is dense and heavy, so humid that you seem to be pushing through it. All the vegetation appears to be wet, and mosquitoes flourish in the stagnant, steamy atmosphere. But I have found my trips very rewarding. The channels through the tall, reed-like "pit-pit" swamp grass are the haunts of a great host of waterbirds. On one occasion I motored slowly along a sinuous waterway observing the birds. Eight pied herons on a log looked about apprehensively at my approach and decided to fly off along the channel ahead of me. Some flew up and over the grass and disappeared, but others joined the birds flying just ahead of me, and soon there were 50 or more of them. Some little black cormorants were swimming and fishing in the channel, and these joined the herons. Egrets, too, joined the flock and we continued like this until the channel opened into a small lagoon. Here the birds dispersed.

Several times in this area I have seen pheasant coucals, surely one of the most ungainly and awkward birds alive. They have poor powers of

flight and the way they flap laboriously into the swamp grass and flop there gives the impression that their evolution stopped 50 million years ago, before they had a chance to become well co-ordinated birds.

Overhead there seems to be a constant traffic of birds from dawn to dusk. Moving along the Ramu-Sepik waterways, with the sunset reflected on the glass-smooth water, herons gliding overhead, and the flowering heads of the pit-pit silver in the evening light—these are grand moments for which I would readily sacrifice a little comfort.

In the south the swamplands of the Purari river delta are comparatively pleasant to visit. It is amazing that in an area of swamp covering nearly two million acres there are so few mosquitoes. This is probably because much of the Purari delta water is constantly on the move, being less restricted in its journey to the sea than the Ramu-Sepik swamp waters. The Purari, after meandering across the alluvial lowlands at about eight knots, breaks up into hundreds of channels. Joined by two other rivers, the Kikori and Era, it spreads its waters into a vast expanse of mud islands, dense swamp forest, sage swamps and *nypa* palm swamps. A delicate balance is maintained in the delta between fresh water brought down from the mountains and sea water mixing with it, and the varying salinity encourages the growth of different types of plants with their dependent forms of wildlife.

Most of the Purari delta is wilderness, for only the fringes have been occupied by native tribes or visited by Europeans. In the depths of the swamps bloom beautiful orchids that would gladden any naturalist. Brilliant birds and butterflies make a kaleidoscope of colour against the sombre greens and greys of the swamp. In parts the interior is impenetrable by man. Close-set palms hedge the waterways and underneath is slimy mud: deep, black, squelchy mud, pitted with crab holes. In the murky waters live snakes, sawfishes and crocodiles. The swampland guards its treasures well.

I have visited the Purari swamps many times. I usually go by motor boat into one of the narrow waterways, then cut the engine and let the craft drift with the tide or push it gently along with a paddle, hoping to glimpse some of the inhabitants: a crab-eating possum, a beautiful green python, or perhaps a flash of azure which is a passing kingfisher.

I remember vividly the plants and animals I saw on one of my visits. It was an unscheduled drift, because the outboard motor had broken down. So while the helmsman tinkered with the engine, we floated down a winding channel. From a distance the muddy banks seemed to be blossoming with tiny red and yellow flags. As we drifted closer I identi-

A lagoon at the foot of Little Mount Lawes is a reminder of the heavy rains that convert savannah to swampland during the wet season.

fied these as colonies of purplish-brown male fiddler crabs, brandishing the coloured claws that are their distinguishing feature. One claw is much larger than the other and is waved up and down in a menacing fashion as the crab sidles along, usually sifting mud through its mouthparts for food at the same time. Hopping about among the crabs were mudskippers—those curious fish with protruding, swivelling eyes and the ability to lead an amphibious life. Their gill openings are small, so that the fish can store water in their branchial chambers to keep the gills wet with sufficient oxygenated water. I noticed a number of them simply resting on a mudbank, tails in the water, while others had pulled themselves up on to palm fronds and were basking there before diving back into the swamp.

Now and then temporary shade from the sun was provided by the overhanging branches of forest trees, and these were festooned with ferns and orchids, many in full flower. I identified *Bulbophyllum grandiflorum* with its single buttercup-yellow blooms, and *Dendrobium smilliae* with its bottlebrush-shaped clump of flowers, each with a round, glossy green centre which explains its popular name of "jellybean orchid". Just ahead of the boat I could see something big lying on one branch. As we came closer I recognized it as a Salvadori's lizard, about 12 feet long. This is a massive goanna, or monitor lizard, which looks much like the Komodo dragon of Indonesia, although it is not so bulky since most of the body consists of a whip-like tail.

It is one of the reptile's favourite habits to lie along branches. After foraging on the forest floor, where it detects odours of possible prey through its sensitive tongue tip, the Salvadori's lizard climbs into a tree over a forest trail. There it waits in ambush. When a ground bird, rat, bandicoot, wallaby or lizard comes along, it is poised to drop on its victim. When hunting in grassland, this reptile will sometimes lift its head and even stand on its hind legs to reconnoitre before going on, poking into logs and tussocks. If cornered, it hisses angrily with the explosive sound of escaping steam, transforming itself into a fierce adversary with lashing tail, huge claws and sharp-pointed teeth. But in general it is much more placid than the smaller goannas.

This one saw us and raised its head. It made a dash for the bank but slipped off the branch in its haste and fell into the water with a heavy splash, swimming across to the protection of a clump of *nypa* palms. The noise of its escape disturbed a flock of red-cheeked parrots feeding in the tops of the trees. Although they were largely obscured by the foliage, their noisy chatter pinpointed their position. As I peered through the gaps in the tree canopy I saw the black shape of a palm cockatoo, a clownish-looking bird with a huge bill, bright red skin on its cheeks, and a high spreading crest of thin black feathers. He was sitting in the centre of a young betel-nut palm, and poked his head up to look at me. His crest, spread out like a miniature palm, repeated the pattern of the surrounding fronds and made him appear ridiculous.

The birds flew off and the noise drifted away. I watched the crabs and mudskippers for a while, and was then diverted by the antics of a shoal of archer fish. The fish is deep-bodied and grows up to a foot long. Its mouth and pharynx are specially modified so that, by contracting the gill-covers and raising the floor of its mouth, it can squirt a jet of water through a groove along the top of its mouth and through a hole in its pursed lips to a distance of ten or 12 feet. The archer fish floats tail down in the water, its body hidden and its lips at water level. With its large movable eyes it searches for a target on the overhanging foliage and then manoeuvres into position, pointing its body at the victim. The fish prefers to squirt its jet vertically; at an oblique angle the chances of miscalculating the aim are increased. Moreover, if the fish is directly under its prey, there is less chance of a rival snapping up the insect as it falls. To lessen the effect of minor errors in marksmanship, the jet of water fans out to cover the target area like grape-shot; and the archer fish can splatter an insect with a salvo of half a dozen or so shots, fired in quick succession, so that its victim seldom escapes.

Eventually we moved out into a wider part of the channel and my helmsman got the engine going again. As we prepared to make up for lost time I looked up and saw a whistling kite gliding serenely overhead. From where we were I could see as far as the sea in one direction, and upstream as far as the distant hazy mountains, the spine of this country and the source of these rivers and wild swamplands.

Voyager to the "Land of Enchantment"

On April 9, 1872, Luigi D'Albertis, an Italian explorer, wrote in his diary: "A memorable day! At last I tread the mysterious land. At last, leaping on shore this morning, I exclaimed, 'We are in New Guinea!'"

The island had been known to the Portuguese since 1562 and several expeditions had visited its coasts. But D'Albertis was the first European to penetrate any distance into its daunting interior. As well as taking an interest in botany, zoology and anthropology, he was also a crack shot—a necessary, and accepted, qualification for a naturalist of those days, before there was much concern about the extinction of entire species: it was usually impossible to preserve live specimens, so they had to be killed on the spot and made into study skins.

Reaching the north-western tip of New Guinea in April, 1872, D'Albertis marched inland for about 20 miles. But ill-health forced him to withdraw to Australia and it was not until 1875 that he returned. This time he headed for Yule Island, in the Gulf of Papua, making it his base during the next three years for frequent excursions into the interior.

Like most 19th-Century explorers, D'Albertis took along an assortment of trinkets to win local favour. Other items from his stock in trade were more original. On one occasion he charmed the tribesmen with kisses; on another, he impressed them by kissing the head of a live snake.

Sailing in the *Neva*, a nine-ton steam-launch provided by the New South Wales government, D'Albertis became the first explorer to travel the full navigable length of the Fly river, some 580 miles. He named its tributary, the Alice, after the wife of the New South Wales premier, and the Victor Emanuel Mountains, in honour of the King of Italy. But the people of the Fly river region were hostile, and in one fierce encounter the *Neva* was struck by 45 arrows.

In 1878 D'Albertis returned to Italy, where his unique collection of specimens won him wide acclaim. The diary recording his adventures and scientific observations was published in Italian and English, and abridged extracts from it appear on the following pages, together with some of the original illustrations, by an unknown artist. The diary sold well, but D'Albertis rejected acclaim, preferring the solitude of the Pontine Marshes. Here he built a replica of a Papuan house as a reminder of New Guinea's "land of enchantment".

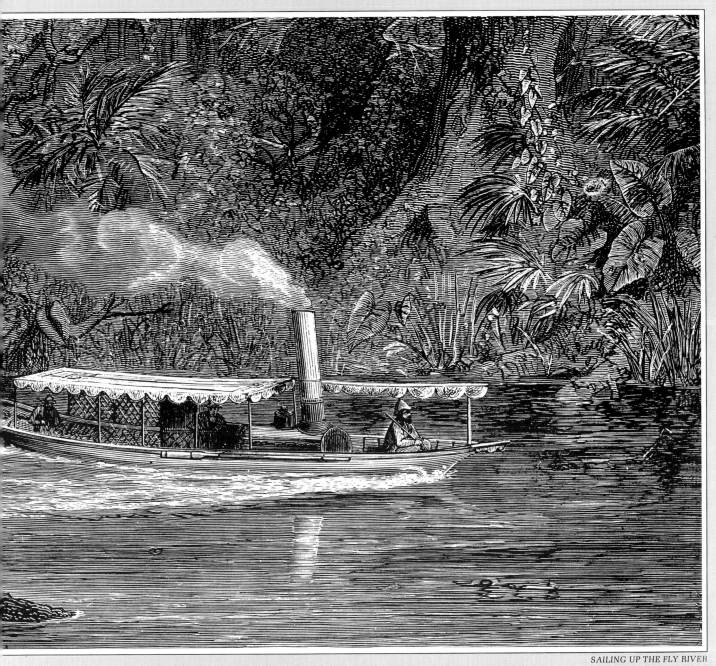

SAILING UP THE FLY RIVER

D'Albertis in New Guinea

LUIGI D'ALBERTIS

It was a real pleasure to me to walk a little on dry land, after having passed so many days at sea, and all the greater because the land was Papua, the country of my dreams. At last I was roaming through a primeval forest, in a free country which had never as yet owned a master.

I was so pleased at finding myself in a primeval forest that I wanted to run about everywhere. But I suffered for my inexperienced impulse; now a thorn pierced my clothes and tore my skin; now a liana, stretched across my path, would throw me down, gun in hand, damaging my hands and knees, and putting me in peril of my life from the gun; again, a spider's web, which had widely spread its insidious snares, would cling to my face and beard, while the spiders fell on my hands, neck and face, producing a singularly unpleasant sensation.

After a ramble of several hours, I had to acknowledge that, in spite of all my dreams, a primeval forest is not the earthly paradise.

Above the ground

The house in which I am at present is 3,500 feet above sea level, on the slopes of a mountain. The house is tolerably large, built on piles, and raised high above the ground. After dinner I went out and, ascending a little hill at the rear of the house, I shot two or three birds; among them one which

I believed to be a young *Parotia sexpennis,* one of the most beautiful birds of paradise known, but of which no specimen has as yet been brought to Europe, except in the shape of greatly mutilated skins, prepared by the natives. Here was another proof that we had come to

HARPYOPSIS WITH PREY

the land of the rare birds of paradise, and now that I am here at last I am absolutely determined to remain!

Tribal warfare

I have to record something serious. The head man of this village told me that his people were at war with another tribe, and that I should be killed if I remained here any longer. I have then only five more days to remain in a country where every shot brings down a bird of a new species, and where every insect I pick up is also new to me. Words cannot depict the bitterness of my mortification at having to bow my head before a greater power! But what could I possibly do alone here?

Words of magic

This morning I crossed from Yule Island to the mainland, and my first shot killed a tree kangaroo. While passing a small brook I shot two ducks, and with my third shot I brought down a fine hawk, which was standing on a trunk of a tree devouring the flesh of a small kangaroo. This splendid bird belongs to a newly discovered genus, namely the *Harpyopsis,* and is approximate to a genus which is found in South America. But at first I did not appreciate its rarity, and went on continually asking the natives why birds of paradise did not appear.

At last my servants had recourse to incantation. The three of them halted, formed as it were a triangle, broke off some small boughs and began to make signs, and utter words of magic, calling several animals by name, and among them birds of paradise. By a strange coincidence ten minutes had not elapsed before we came to a tree on which I was delighted to see three full-grown birds of paradise, and killed the two finest.

A beautiful species

The natives are not only quiet, but are working for me and bring in a good number of birds killed with arrows. They have also brought me a few mammiferous animals and frogs. Among the mammiferous animals I may mention a beautiful new species of cuscus (the pentailed phalanger), which is much esteemed by the natives for its flesh. The top of its tail is also used by them to make ear-rings.

PENTAILED PHALANGER

With some guides I arrived at a remote village on the summit of a hill and the largest house was placed at my disposal. At dusk several other men and women arrived in the village, on their return from hunting the grey dorcopsis, of which they had killed 20. They use long nets in hunting this animal, with which they surround its haunts, and when it is entangled in the nets they kill it with clubs.

The chief of the village is called Aira, and towards evening I was summoned in haste to his house, where I found him, spear in hand. A huge serpent was trailing itself slowly along with Aira making frantic signs at it.

My guides, who did not know the snake was tame and that it belonged to Aira, tried to kill it before I could prevent them, but fortunately the reptile made good its escape. Aira was fuming with rage and began to vent his wrath by thrusting with his spear at an old coconut lying near his feet. At that moment he looked like a terrible and wrathful sorcerer. My native companions were quite dismayed and when night fell took themselves into a corner and were plotting something.

My time for action had now come, and taking a large handful of gunpowder, I strewed it on the ground. One of the natives, who was in my confidence, applied fire to it without anyone perceiving what he did. The bright flash and the suffocating smoke combined to produce an immense effect.

When tranquillity appeared to be restored, I went to Aira's house and calmed his ire, which had already much subsided. Now all is still, but I do not think it prudent to sleep without my revolver by my side.

GREY DORCOPSIS

MAINLAND NEW GUINEA FROM YULE ISLAND

When I returned to Yule Island from the mainland, a servant brought me the news that the natives had broken into the house in the night and carried off all they could. Fortunately, I had secreted some guns, cartridges and dynamite. I told the natives that if my property was not restored within 24 hours I would fire at everyone who came within range of my guns. In the meantime, I had put all my guns into good order, loaded some Orsini shells, and mined the paths leading to the house so that, with a long match, I could blow them up without going out or exposing myself to danger.

I then took a tin case and loaded it with dynamite, and closing it tightly, fired it. The detonation which followed was like the roar of a cannonade, and the echoes resounded for several seconds. I then let off rockets in the direction of the natives' houses. When day broke, six villagers came back up the path bringing some of the stolen goods. They trembled like half-drowned rats, and said the women had fled the island.

The women, although obliged to work hard, are held in respect, and in

A PAPUAN VILLAGE

some villages they exercise much authority and power. I am inclined to think that a community composed of women would never be attacked by another tribe. Women in New Guinea act, in short, like a banner of peace.

Operatic recital

The natives, allured by the amount I pay for the animals they bring me, have all made themselves collectors for my sake, and today I have been compelled to decline a good many reptiles, on account of having exhausted my store of spirits of wine, and having no other means of preserving them.

The women are my great friends. They were greatly astonished at my petroleum lamp and I taught them how to supply themselves with lamp-light by using the fat of animals.

To keep them in good humour and amuse them, I sang for them in the evening some airs from Italian operas, and collected the whole population in front of my house. My success was immense. I was applauded and compelled to repeat some of the pieces which pleased them most. I ought to confess, however, that I should not venture to sing in any other country than New Guinea.

Order and cleanliness

The people live in communities, sometimes of more than a thousand inhabitants, in well-built villages, worthy to be called small towns, both for their order and cleanliness. The houses are built on pillars composed of large tree trunks at about

"MUSICAL" SKULL

EMBALMED HEAD

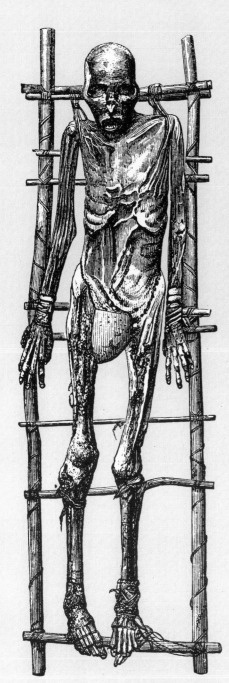

DARNLEY ISLAND MUMMY

six feet from the ground. Some of these trunks are roughly carved. The houses are spacious, with a very high, pointed roof, like an upside-down hull of a boat.

Preserving the dead

I was very much pleased at being able to land on Darnley Island. The island presents an enchanting view from the sea, with its summits clad in bright green and with its valleys where the lovely palm coconut and bamboo flourish.

The natives are not nude, but slightly clothed with leaves and grass. They appear to venerate their dead, and preserve them by embalming and desiccation. I saw the corpse thus preserved of the husband of one of the prettiest women, he having been dead over a year. He still occupied the nuptial chamber, standing in the middle of the house attached to a kind of upright ladder.

Equally remarkable were 14 skulls found in a village near the Fly river. They were covered by a sort of half mask representing a face, which appears to be made of a resinous wax, and is adorned by seeds and shells. The nostrils and eyes are made of shells. To judge from their whole aspect, and also from some small stones and beads, these skulls

must be used as instruments of music, or rather, of noise.

Another curiosity was the embalmed head of a man with nothing remaining on it but the skin, from which the skull had been removed by means of a long cut at the back. The skin had afterwards been stuffed in such a way as to retain the natural appearance of a head. It has the defect of being too much stuffed and is alike horrible and ridiculous.

Savagery and sorrow

I cannot but deplore the barbarity of some of these people. In one village from which the inhabitants fled at our approach, we found an old woman with her skull driven in. My men told me that, on account of her blind and dying condition, her own people had ended her life to prevent her falling into our hands.

And yet, are they complete savages? Once, when a boy died in a house near mine, the parents' lamentations were heart-rending. A grave about three feet deep was dug in front of the house, and into this the mortal remains of the child were laid. As soon as the grave was filled up, the poor mother, and shortly afterwards the father, too, prostrated themselves on it, and lay there through the night and following day.

Today the Italian flag was hoisted on the Fly river, and united with the flag of New South Wales. When looking at the flags, I thought of those two countries. I am a son of the first, the second is loved by me as a second fatherland. When I saw the two flags hoisted together, they seemed to me two sisters, and from my heart I desired that the nations whom they represent should call themselves brethren.

Undiscovered treasures

I cannot understand why the natives attack us. Our launch, the *Neva*, steers well clear of their villages. I would be friendly, not only from humane, but also from interested motives, for experience has taught me how useful the natives are in assisting a naturalist to form his collections. How many treasures I might have obtained from these people, which will now remain unknown for many years! What an advantage it would be for the natives to understand how many benefits they might derive from our acquaintance! But no, they come with the intention of killing us.

Forerunners of bloodshed

Morning dawned slowly, the sun lacked power to dissipate the dark veil of night. At last day broke, but the round, rayless sun showed itself through the fog, which it was unable to disperse, a crimson disc. The land and the forest appeared, little by little, but were still wrapped in mist.

While we, wet and shivering, were waiting to start, five large hawks, like spectres of the night, whirled about in the air above our heads, now near, now far from us. I said: "These hawks are forerunners of bloodshed; they have already scented corpses."

After we had steamed about five miles in the fog, the look-out shouted "Canoes in front!" I looked and saw threescore and a half men in their canoes, armed with bows and arrows and with diabolical noises, attacking us and trying to bar our way. We made as quickly as possible for the left bank, trying to proceed without giving or receiving any bodily harm, but coming within bowshot, they began to shoot at the *Neva*.

One canoe only, with a solitary man in it, came within range of our guns. He put down his paddle, took up his bow, and the arrow passed over my head. Three shots made him fall in the river and disappear. I must say, the natives evinced courage.

The genii appear

There has been a furious wind, lightning, thunderbolts, and a complete deluge of rain. While we were trying to re-anchor, two birds of paradise slowly crossed the river, and during the day many more perched on the neighbouring trees; but we were too tired to pay any heed.

I hear their note almost daily and it has always fascinated me. But now I am bidding farewell to the wild country, it sounds sweeter than ever in my ears. It seems to invite me to stay. The birds are like the genii of the place, saying: Leave us not.

THE NEVA UNDER ATTACK

6/ Volcanoes in the Sea

At the northern end of New Britain, the largest of New Guinea's offshore islands, there is a semi-circular bay, like an amphitheatre filled with water. It is known as Blanche Bay and is the site of Rabaul, once the capital of the Mandated Territory of New Guinea. In the bay there was an island that the German administration of New Britain before the First World War had named Vulcan. At the beginning of 1937 Vulcan was a low, pear-shaped island with a shallow, water-filled crater one to two hundred yards in diameter at its south-western corner; it was not to retain this appearance for much longer.

On Friday, May 28 that year, the residents of Rabaul felt a series of earth tremors which increased in severity during the day. Earthquakes are common in the offshore islands, and since the tremors ceased towards nightfall, preparations continued for a special "sing-sing", a colourful dance and feast which was to be held the following day. The island of Vulcan lay silent in Blanche Bay as it had done for decades past and on the opposite side of the bay the familiar wisp of steam coiled up into the evening sky from the dormant volcano Matupit.

The next morning the sea near Vulcan was boiling and shoals of dead fish floated on the surface. People were coming to Rabaul for the sing-sing, and by afternoon hundreds watched the spectacle of the boiling sea water from the near-by hillsides. The volcanic activity built up to a climax: Vulcan gave a heave and exploded with a tremendous roar, sending a column of fumes, rocks and ash hurtling thousands of feet into the air like an atomic mushroom cloud. Ash and pumice rained upon Rabaul, weighing down the trees in the streets, covering gardens and pounding ships in the bay.

Vulcan had proved itself to be a volcano. With the outpourings of ash and rock, the new volcano grew in size, intermittently exploding with loud reports that resounded over the countryside. In the early afternoon of Sunday, May 30, the dormant volcano Matupit, across the bay from Rabaul, erupted without warning, adding its fumes to those of Vulcan. Throughout the day both old and new volcanoes sent columns of hot ash high into the air. Blanche Bay became a sea of pumice. As darkness fell, a thunderstorm hit the area, possibly brought on by the heat of the eruptions. Sheets of lightning slashed across the bay, mixing with the fires from the two volcanoes and adding to the terror of the scene.

By the fourth day, the low island of Vulcan had become a cone more than 700 feet high, with steam issuing steadily from its peak. During the eruptions two villages on the shore had been buried under ash blowing north-westward from Vulcan and 507 people lost their lives. In Rabaul the inhabitants began the task of cleaning up the ash, which lay in a layer between three and six inches thick, and both volcanoes quickly quietened down until they were no more than steaming cauldrons, as Matupit had been before. Flying over Blanche Bay recently, I looked down on the dormant cone of Matupit and at Vulcan, now no longer an island but incorporated within the shoreline. It was incredible to think that this peak thickly covered with forest had come into existence such a short time ago.

Yet Vulcan is only one of hundreds of volcanoes which have risen from the sea around New Guinea in the last few million years. Numerous small islands are scattered in the offshore waters, and many are the peaks of half-drowned volcanoes. Some have an active cone with two or three older, silent cones alongside. Some are merely the blown-out shells of volcanoes long extinct. Others have sunk beneath the waves and have either disappeared from view or are identified only by the coral cays that have grown on top of them.

Nevertheless, Vulcan is of particular interest, since its recent eruption demonstrates how quickly new land can be formed by volcanic action and pinpoints one of the most active centres of geological change in Papua New Guinea. Vulcan is only the latest in a long series of volcanoes which have sprung up on this site. Blanche Bay is itself the remnant of a giant volcanic crater, and a clutch of younger volcanoes has hatched around its rim, including several cones which are now extinct, in addition to the active ones of Vulcan and Matupit.

There is good reason for this concentration of volcanoes. Blanche Bay lies at the junction of two great oceanic trenches, one hugging the southern shore of New Britain, the other running along the western shore of Bougainville and down through the Solomon Islands. These trenches are the tell-tale signs of geological cataclysm, for they mark the destructive plate margins where one section of the earth's crust is being forced down, or subducted, beneath another. The trenches are far bigger physical features than the mountains of New Guinea. The New Britain Trench plummets to a depth exceeding 24,000 feet below sea level, far deeper than the largest New Guinea mountains are high.

It is here, along these trenches, that the margins of the Pacific Ocean floor are breaking up. Each trench represents only the first fraction of a descending plate's journey into the earth's mantle. Over a period of many millennia the plate will be forced down 50 miles or more before it begins to melt and be mixed into the hot mass of the earth's mantle. This great geological process is accompanied by the severe earthquakes and frequent volcanic eruptions that the islanders know only too well.

More people have been killed by volcanic action in the West Pacific and Indonesia than in any other region on earth. In 1883 the eruption of Krakatoa, 2,000 miles west of New Guinea, caused 35,000 deaths. One reason for such high mortality figures is that in island arcs such as the New Britain and Solomon archipelagos, the magma is composed not of basalt, as for example in Iceland, but mainly of andesite. The viscosity of basalt magma is low, and the gases trapped within it can escape freely, spraying off into the air as "fire fountains" and causing comparatively few casualties. Andesite, however, has a high viscosity. Dissolved gas trapped within it can blast free only in violent explosions.

The eruption of Vulcan was a typical andesitic explosion, but in 1951 a much more lethal andesitic eruption occurred on the mainland of Papua New Guinea. Local people in the Northern Province claimed that their ancestors had seen smoke issuing from Mount Lamington, but no one suspected the mountain was a volcano. Geologists had no reason to pay attention to the local folk story since smoke may be observed on any mountain where fires have been lit; more important, there was no obvious geological evidence to provide a clue.

When Mount Lamington erupted, it did so in the worst form of volcanic activity: a *nuée ardente* or burning cloud. This effect is created by an explosion of gases trapped under tremendous pressure within

In New Britain, vegetation has colonized the rain-furrowed lower slopes of Matupit's cone and is slowly enveloping the volcano's rim.

viscous, nearly solid magma. In the case of Mount Lamington, a cloud of superheated gas, volcanic dust and lava fragments raced down the mountainside at almost 60 miles an hour, scorching to death more than 3,000 people, most of them inhabitants of Higaturu, a town at the foot of the mountain. Many hundreds more were seriously burned.

It is surprising that such an eruption should have occurred on the mainland, since most of New Guinea's volcanoes are clustered in the offshore islands, especially New Britain and Bougainville, where subduction is taking place. However, in an area as geologically complex as this, many things are possible. The eruption of Mount Lamington and the presence of other vents on the north side of the island may indicate that a new subduction zone is forming along the north-east coast and that a section of ocean crust is beginning to plunge beneath the mainland of New Guinea, with all the attendant upheavals.

More significant from an everyday point of view is the unexpected nature of the Lamington eruption. With so many gently steaming volcanoes in New Guinea there is always a chance that human life will be lost in an eruption somewhere. Although nowadays vulcanologists can sometimes predict where and when violent activity is going to occur, volcanoes nevertheless often behave in unpredictable ways. In spite of technical advances, volcanoes are still untamed by man, and whether they are found in remote or populated areas, on land or in the sea, they remain among the wildest phenomena in nature.

Even as I write, a report is coming over the radio about renewed volcanic activity on Karkar Island, ten miles off Madang on the north coast. I have visited many of New Guinea's offshore islands, including several that are active volcanoes. It was not long ago that I explored Karkar. The island is one huge volcano, nearly circular and about 12 miles in diameter. It rises from the ocean floor 3,000 feet below sea level. I went to Karkar in the company of a herpetologist from Australia. He was an old friend of mine, and I joined him to collect local artifacts for the museum in Port Moresby while he collected reptiles in each of the island's three vegetation levels.

As we approached Karkar from the sea, escorted by a school of dolphins, we saw that the lower slopes were covered by native gardens and coconut plantations. Above this cultivated area was a belt of thick bush leading to a high-canopied forest. The trees extended almost to the top of the volcano but there was a wide gap near the peak from which we could clearly trace the path where a broad stream of lava had once flowed down into the ocean. As we neared the shore we saw the waves washing over shining, jagged slabs of solidified lava. The density of plant cover testified to the richness of the volcanic soil on the mountain slopes and suggested that there was a profusion of animal life there as well, with ample concealment for frogs, lizards and snakes.

My work with the people of the island was soon done. Little remained of the traditional local culture, although I was shown the immense *garumut* drums owned by every village community. Each drum was a section of log six to ten feet long and about three feet in diameter. On one end was carved a stylized head representing an ancestral protective spirit. Along the top of the log, which was laid lengthways across two small supporting logs, was a slit some four inches wide. Through this slit much of the inside of the log had been chipped out with adzes. One or two heavy sticks were used to thump across the slit or to one side. I was given a demonstration, and the booming noise that resulted could, I am sure, be heard more than a mile away. In fact, I was told that one giant *garumut* drum at the southern end of the island could be used to send signals across to the mainland at Matuka, more than 12 miles away.

I was soon able to join my friend in his research on reptiles and amphibians. We were anxious to see the upper slopes and the volcano's crater, so we prepared our gear and recruited a few carriers, planning to camp near the summit for a couple of days.

We had not climbed far beyond the cultivated levels before we encountered our first unusual animal. A few old coconut husks were lying beside the track and out from behind one of these scuttled a strange-looking lizard with a hard, triangular head and three rows of serrated scales down the back. It was only about six inches long and resembled a prehistoric monster in miniature. My friend immediately identified it as an armoured spiny-tailed skink, pointing out that because of its drab, dark brown body, it usually camouflages itself by lying motionless among the leaves and rocks of the forest floor.

About half an hour later we came across a rather more dangerous customer, a greyish-brown death adder, slithering into a crevice under a slab of black rock. The remarkable thing about this snake is that instead of actively seeking prey it waits for its victim to come within range. Detecting the scent of a fresh animal trail by touching the ground with its sensitive tongue tip, the adder coils up and lies motionless, leaving its tail just in front of its head. The tip of the adder's tail is creamy white, contrasting with the grey, brown or ochre colour of the rest of the body, and resembles a grub or caterpillar. To reinforce the illusion, the adder wiggles the tail tip. Attracted by what appears to be a tasty morsel, the potential victim—a mouse, bird, frog or lizard—ventures to within striking distance of the snake's jaws. Poison fangs almost a quarter of an inch long instantly inject powerful neurotoxic venom into the prey and death results within seconds.

Collecting a number of small reptiles and amphibians as we climbed, we found a campsite about 500 feet below the rim of the crater, beside an old lava flow where a small creek trickled down from pool to pool in the contorted surface. A little way downstream the creek disappeared underground. Here the lava flow had covered a thick layer of old volcanic ash, and when the water broke through, it had eaten away the ash, forming small caves. In some of these caves we found the nests of glossy swiftlets, common throughout the south-west Pacific, clinging to the underside of the lava flow.

After setting up camp we wandered a little way down the track and collected more reptiles, including two interesting snakes. One was the harmless slaty-grey snake, whose belly has sharply angled sides to help it climb trees. The other snake had to be treated with considerable care. This was a venomous, three-foot, small-eyed snake, with a black head and a striking colour pattern of black bands across a peach-pink background. It is a common species on Karkar and is greatly feared by the islanders, even more so than the death adder: its bite has caused a number of fatalities.

The slopes of Karkar tend to be shrouded in heavy mist by about mid-day, so we rose early next morning in order to get to the crater in clear weather. It took us about an hour and a half to climb the last 500 feet to its edge, and the mists still held off. I had a mental picture of a crater as a bare expanse devoid of life; but when we reached the top I found this one was quite different. It was more than a mile in diameter. The sides were almost sheer and covered with mosses and ferns dripping with water. The floor was a relatively flat expanse of grass and shrubs, but in places there were bare patches of uneven black lava and pumice. The carriers told us that these spots were warm, too warm to stand on for long, and that was why no grass or shrubs grew there.

I scanned the crater with binoculars. The walls were from 500 to 1,200 feet high and looked unscaleable, but the carriers said there were two tracks down. However, clouds were already gathering and we did not descend since we would soon have been unable to see our way. A bit off-centre in the crater was the cone of a second, newer volcano—a cone within a cone. It was well forested with medium-high trees, grasses,

A Polynesian blue-tailed skink sits motionless and alert in the undergrowth on Karkar Island. When attacked, this five-inch long lizard sheds its tail, which continues to writhe, distracting the predator while the skink makes good its escape. Unlike some other skinks, which have blue tails only when they are young, the Polynesian blue-tailed skink retains this safety device throughout its life, and quickly grows a new tail to replace the one it has shed.

shrubs and mosses, and as far as I could make out through my binocu-lars it had a depression at the top—its own little crater.

I stood on the very rim of the main crater and looked about. Far to the north-west I could see the island volcano of Manam over which I had flown during an eruption. There is a legend on Karkar Island that if Manam were to cease its activity, Karkar would erupt. In fact, Manam has not ceased erupting; but since my visit Karkar has had several minor eruptions, sending out fumes, gases, ash and rock, and the small cone I saw has been much altered in appearance. I could not study Manam for long. A huge bank of cloud advanced to Karkar's crater, poured over the edge and tumbled downwards. As we turned and made our way back to camp, we were enveloped in mist.

After descending from the volcano's rim we stayed for a couple of days in a house on the coast, attending to the collections we had made and writing up our notes. I remember walking about a room one day and feeling a bit unsteady, and I put it down to a touch of the sun. Next day when a government officer came to see us, he asked if we had felt the *guria*, or tremor, and I realized that I had experienced evidence of Karkar's continuing activity.

The tree-clad island volcanoes of New Guinea, which rise hundreds or even thousands of feet above sea level, are usually regarded as being distinct from the coral islands and atolls—which usually are mere rings or horse-shoes of sand encircling a lagoon. However, the difference is more apparent than real, for many coral islands once were volcanoes. The first to realize this was Charles Darwin who, in the course of his voy-age around the world in the *Beagle*, examined a number of coral atolls in mid-ocean. Knowing that corals normally flourish only in shallow water, he suggested that coral atolls in deep sea areas had originally been established as fringing reefs around island volcanoes. As the islands sank down to sea level, probably as a result of internal movements, coral grew all over them. Gradually the volcanoes subsided below the surface, and the coral grew rapidly enough to keep pace and remain at the surface. The existence of such volcanic foundations has been proved in places by deep drilling.

The coral islands vary from tiny platforms with no soil or vegetation to story-book "desert islands". The Trobriand Islands, a group of raised coral shelves only 60 to 70 feet high about a hundred miles off the eastern tip of New Guinea, appear to be ideal desert islands: they have palm trees, thatched houses, outrigger canoes, beautiful girls, coral reefs, long beaches and wonderful fishing. Inland, away from the villages, it is a different story. The forest is straggly and meagre since the soil is too thin to support many big trees. The trees that do grow tend to be twisted and gnarled; there are dense thickets of low shrubs and thin saplings about ten feet high. It is awful terrain to penetrate and often the jagged points of the underlying coral trip you up and tear your boots.

But although the vegetation may look poor, it is teeming with animal life. I have never seen so many eclectus parrots as there are on these islands. They are usually in pairs in the treetops and they keep up a loud, shrill screeching as if everyone down below were after them. On several occasions I have caught glimpses of one of New Guinea's largest monitor lizards, the spotted goanna. This reptile grows to at least six feet in length and, like all monitors, possesses sharp teeth and claws. A specimen which has just shed its skin is particularly attractive: rich black and finely spotted with yellow. The islanders consider the goanna's meat a delicacy, and use the skin to cover their hourglass-shaped drums, known as *kundus*. Still, with all the hunting that goes on, the monitor lizard population remains quite large.

Off the coasts of the mainland and the chief islands in the Bismarck Archipelago and Admiralty Islands many coral islets provide breeding grounds for seabirds, and occasionally for landbirds. Terns nest in their hundreds, and it is thought that when more of the islands are investigated, gannet rookeries and mutton bird warrens will be discovered. Seagulls are not found in New Guinea except as stragglers from Australia. I have visited several of the islets and watched the activities of noddy terns, black-naped terns, bridled terns, reef herons and also Pacific swallows, which glue their cup-shaped nests of mud to the undersides of coral ledges. Offshore many of the seabirds glide about, diving into the clear waters around the coral reefs for food.

I am always cautious on these islets, for they are the habitat of one of New Guinea's deadly snakes—the black and white banded sea snake, one of the few species of sea snake that come out of the water to rest and breed. I have often watched them while swimming along a reef with an aqualung. They crawl in and out of cavities in the coral in search of small eels and reef fish. After a while they rise to the surface of the sea to breathe, then wriggle quickly down again to continue their hunting. The offshore islands are also used for breeding by the green turtle which, like the hawksbill turtle, is common around the New Guinea coasts. The sandy beaches provide suitable nests for the turtles to lay their eggs. On the inhabited islands the local people eat the eggs; and although formerly

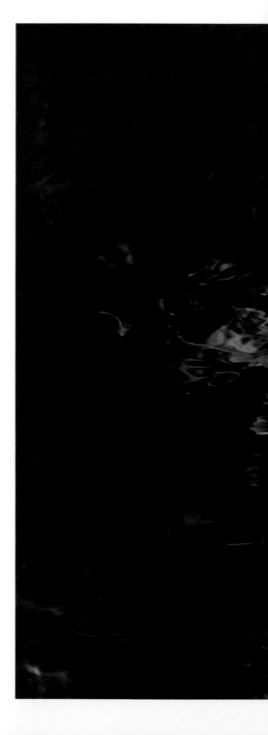

A catfish scavenges off the New Guinea coast. The whisker-like barbels around its mouth are sensitive feelers that supplement its poor vision.

they collected only enough for their own needs, they now sell eggs in addition to the turtle shells, which are popular as ornaments. This growing trade is taking a heavy toll of the turtle population.

Some of the offshore islands provide safe breeding grounds for land birds. Nicobar pigeons are found on the islets off Manus Island in the Admiralty group. They are handsome birds with iridescent green and green-brown hackle plumes. When I visited Grange Island, off the south-east coast of Papua near Amazon Bay, I found a variety of visitors, including white-headed kingfishers and rainbow bee-eaters—birds that do not usually breed here. I also found some Torres Strait pigeons nesting on the island. The Torres Strait pigeon is one of several local species of imperial or nutmeg pigeons, so called because many of the species feed on nutmegs or other large nuts and fruits. These pigeons are big, black and white birds that congregate in large flocks. Each pair was guarding a single egg, laid on a platform of thin sticks, and some of the birds were shuttling to and from the mainland to feed.

To the north of New Guinea there are many islands where hot springs and their spouting counterparts, geysers, can be found. Hot springs and geysers are heated by contact with volcanic rocks. They usually occur in areas where volcanic activity is declining, but although they are unlikely to develop into major centres of volcanic activity, they are nevertheless dangerous to explore.

These thermal areas provide specialized living conditions for a variety of plants and animals. Among them are those curious birds known as megapodes ("large feet"). They belong to the same order of birds as the fowl and pheasant family (Galliformes); there are seven genera, three confined to Australia, two to New Guinea and two with a wider range that extends to the Philippines. They bear common names such as scrub fowl, brush turkey and mallee fowl. Megapodes incubate their eggs in mounds of leaf litter and humus. This involves a good deal of work: the male builds a nesting mound up to eight feet high and 30 feet across. The female lays single eggs at intervals over a period of several months, and the heat of the fermenting leaves keeps them warm. The temperature of the mound would vary considerably according to the time of day and the weather, but the male bird continually tests the temperature with his tongue and scratches away at the litter or heaps it up again to keep the eggs at the optimum incubating temperature of about 93° Fahrenheit.

The common scrub fowl in New Guinea employs this laborious method, but in New Britain, New Ireland and the Solomon Islands, the local sub-species of scrub fowl have dispensed with the task of mound

Shallow reefs of live coral fringe the shores of Kiriwina, one of the Trobriand Group, lying off the eastern tip of New Guinea. The island's core is volcanic rock which was eroded and slowly subsided below the sea. A coral shelf grew on this laval base, and sand and meagre soil have piled up on the coral.

building and temperature adjustment. Instead, these astute birds dig a burrow up to three feet deep in the warm volcanic soil, and the female deposits her eggs in the burrow, where the temperature remains fairly constant throughout the period of incubation.

Some of the most active thermal regions of New Guinea are found in the D'Entrecasteaux Islands. I visited one of these with some botanists during a two-week trip through the islands by government trawler. This thermal field was one of three on Fergusson Island, largest of the group. We anchored the trawler, *Yelangili*, near a village called Dei Dei. Although the springs were only about 20 minutes' walk from there, we decided to get a guide because there is a real danger in these fields of breaking through the thin crust of sinter (the siliceous or calcareous material forming around hot springs) and stepping into a pool of boiling water or a crevice of super-heated steam. The villagers know the safest tracks, so we asked two local girls to come with us as guides.

Leaving the neatly thatched village, we took a muddy track through waist-high sword grass dotted with small shrubs and tall pandans. I had not realized until then how varied these trees can be. The trunks of the more mature pandans have spiralling bases of old leaves (which is the reason for their alternative name of "screw palm"). In some cases, thick prop roots emerge at an angle from midway up the trunk or from just under the crown, extending straight down to the ground; in others a short fringe of roots protrudes a couple of feet above the ground at the base of the trunk. The pandan's fruit comes in all sizes and shapes from banana-like pods to huge pineapple-like fruits bigger than footballs.

Farther along the track we entered a forest consisting mainly of paper-bark trees. The bark of these trees can be peeled off in thin sheets (hence the name), and the flowers, shaped like bottle brushes, attract several kinds of honeyeaters. As we passed by, a friar bird gave his rollicking, chortling call. He is one of the largest honeyeaters, about 12 inches long, and with his dull brown feathers and bare head, he must also be the plainest. We heard a thin, piping cry at the side of the track which came from a tiny sunbird. In fact there was a pair. The female, a pale yellow and olive bird, was shy; but the male was perched on a branch above our heads, where we could admire his bright yellow feathers and shining black throat. Unlike the honeyeater, with its characteristic brush-like tongue, the sunbird has a long, protrusible tongue whose sides are folded over to form a tube.

There were a few epiphytic orchids clinging to some trees, but a delight for us all were the hosts of beautiful pink ground orchids of the genus

Warm water trickles across a bed of mineral salts in the Pau thermal spring area of West New Britain. Scalding hot when it emerges from the depths, the water cools as it flows above ground. The grey formations in the background are crystalline crusts of dissolved sulphur and other minerals which have been deposited by water over the years.

Spathoglottis. They were the biggest flowers of this group that I had ever seen. The stalks stood hip-high and carried heads of some 12 blooms, each two inches in diameter; some were almost white and others ranged from pink to deep mauve.

Our path led us to the bank of a stream, where I detected wisps of steam coming off the water. We had come to a creek that was fed from the thermal area. A little farther on I noticed the first hot spring, no more than a hole in the bank at water level; it was bubbling away and adding water to the creek. Near by a steady jet of steam hissed out of a crack in the ground. Eventually our path petered out at the base of a broad terraced area of mineral salts, over which poured a slow but steady trickle of water. The terraces were like flights of wide steps with low risers, and the water flowing down them dropped into a deep pool of the palest green. Holes in the floor of the pool and a string of bubbles rising from them indicated where more water was feeding in. The wave of wispy steam that wandered like a wraith over the surface indicated that the water was extemely hot.

At the top of the terrace we emerged on to a stretch of bare ground where dozens of small geysers belched steam and water several feet into the air. I lagged behind to take photographs but was hurried on by our guides who assured me that the "best place" lay ahead. I stopped again where a pool of bubbling mud reminded me of a saucepan of boiling chocolate custard, or perhaps a witch's cauldron. Before I caught up with the rest of the party I walked over a platform of mineral salts which was cracked in many places. I could see that this was a dangerous place to cross: some of the salt deposits covered deep holes of hot water or mud. So I kept to the track until we reached the "best place".

It was indeed spectacular. An area of more than an acre was almost covered with the same terraces of mineral salts and water and there were several large holes in which steam jets roared with a deep, mournful sound. From two of the largest cavities, with tall banks of crystalline formation around the perimeters, geysers of steam and water gushed intermittently at least 25 feet into the air. The larger of the two jets was known as Seuseulina and one of our guides showed us how they "called up" the geyser. Standing a few feet away from the holes she threw in a stone and spoke a few words to the geyser to ask it to come up and perform for us. There was a bubbling noise but no geyser. The girl charmingly turned to us and said that it was asking us to watch. She threw in another stone and up came a spout of boiling water and steam which towered above us for a few seconds and then suddenly collapsed, leaving a white plume of steam which wafted away and vanished into the air. The girl turned to us as if to say "How was that?", and we duly registered our delight and appreciation.

Having watched the geyser spouting half a dozen times, I peered down at a small steam hole in the crystalline crust and there, growing healthily on the edge, was a beautiful young pitcher plant, the pitcher-shaped receptacles hardly bigger than thimbles. Near by, even more surprisingly, was a flower-laden *Melastoma* shrub.

As we turned to leave, I took a last look around. The whole area in its bushland setting gave me the impression that our earth was working off some of its energy. This was a place where it could take breath, so to speak, from the effort of reshaping its crust. I often wonder, during my travels among New Guinea's islands, what this part of the earth's crust will look like in a few million years. Many geologists believe that island arcs are the birthplaces of continents. When two oceanic plates collide and volcanic activity throws up a string of islands, the magma is predominantly andesitic—and andesite magmas produce the comparatively light rocks of which continents are made. As the oceanic plates shuffle around, island arcs are swept up together, just as the ancient New Britain arc was thrown up against palaeo-New Guinea 20 million years ago. One day, hundreds of millions of years hence, all the island arcs in the West Pacific may be joined into one new landmass.

It is a fascinating notion. And whether the prophecy is fulfilled or not, the continuing changes in the earth's crust are a salutary reminder to man of his own insignificance. One slight convulsion, one breath from the fiery bowels of the earth can wipe out a city, raise a new island or destroy a forest. Little else gives man a feeling of such utter helplessness as an earthquake or a volcanic eruption. At such times, man, with all his powers, is cut down to size by nature.

Jewels of the Forest

New Guinea contains 660 known bird species, which is more than the total for the whole of Europe. And these many species include the most brilliantly coloured birds in the world. So spectacular are some of them that they have been given such names as "magnificent bird of paradise" (right) or "superb fruit dove". Most of these birds live in the lowland and mid-mountain forests, and their exotic colours appear in jewel-like glimmers as they dart about among the trees.

The uncommon beauty of these birds has at least two practical purposes. One is propagation. Since visibility is often limited in the forest, the birds' vivid colours serve to advertise their presence to others of their kind. Species recognition is particularly important to birds of paradise, for example. Unlike most other birds, birds of paradise do not pair before mating; so the plumed finery of the males, displayed during the courtship dances, serves to attract the females. "Birds of paradise," wrote one European observer in 1784, "glisten like the seldom glimpsed denizens of an Asiatic harem who are clad in gold of many hues dipped in the purple of dawn."

Oddly, the same vivid colours that serve to attract also function as camouflage amidst the colourful flora of the jungle canopy. Thus a second purpose of the vivid plumage is to reduce the birds' chances of ending up as prey. The superb fruit dove, for example, with its irregular pattern of yellowish green, orange, purple and black feathers, is effectively camouflaged when feeding in the dappled light and shade of the tree canopy. If threatened, it can freeze in place, its colours blending into the varied setting.

MAGNIFICENT BIRD OF PARADISE

SUPERB BIRD OF PARADISE

VICTORIA CROWNED PIGEON

KING BIRD OF PARADISE

SUPERB FRUIT DOVE

COMMON PARADISE KINGFISHER

RAGGIANA BIRD OF PARADISE

RAINBOW BEE-EATER

Bibliography

Archbold, Richard, and Rand, A. L., *Results of the Archbold Expeditions No. 7, Summary of the 1933-34 Papuan Expedition.* Bulletin, American Museum of Natural History, Vol. 68, Art. 8, pp. 527-579, 1935.

Atlas of Papua and New Guinea. University of Papua and New Guinea and Collins, Longman, 1970.

Australian Natural History, Vol. 17, No. 12, 1973.

Bergman, Sten, *My Father is a Cannibal.* Robert Hale, 1961.

Brookfield, H. C., and Hart, Doreen, *Melanesia.* Methuen and Co., 1971.

Chalmers, James, *Pioneering in New Guinea.* The Religious Tract Society, 1887.

D'Albertis, L. M., *New Guinea: What I Did and What I Saw.* Sampson Low, Marston, Searle and Rivington, 1880.

Dampier, William, *A Voyage to New Holland in the Year 1699.* Argonaut Press, 1939.

Diamond, M. Jared, *Avifauna of the Eastern Highlands.* Nuttall Ornithological Club, U.S.A., 1972.

Dictionary of the Generic and Family Names of Flowering Plants, New Guinea and South West Pacific Region. Botany Bulletin No. 3, Division of Botany, Lae, Papua New Guinea, 1969.

Dupeyrat, André, *Papua: Beasts and Men.* Macgibbon and Kee, 1963.

Ford, Edgar, *The Land and the People.* The Jacaranda Press, 1974.

Ford, Edgar, Ed., *Papua New Guinea Resource Atlas.* The Jacaranda Press, 1974.

Frith, H. S., *Waterfowl in Australia.* Angus and Robertson, 1967.

Hastings, P., Ed., *Papua New Guinea—Prospero's Other Island.* Angus and Robertson, 1971.

Gilliard, E. T., *Birds of Paradise and Bower Birds.* Weidenfeld and Nicolson, 1969.

Hilder, Brett, *Navigator in the South Seas.* Percival Marshall and Co., 1961.

Hides, Jack, *Beyond the Kubea.* Angus and Robertson, 1939.

Hides, Jack, *Papuan Wonderland.* Angus and Robertson, 1973.

Iredale, T., *Birds of Paradise and Bower Birds.* Georgian House, 1950.

Jukes, J. Beete, *Narrative of the Surveying Voyage of H.M.S. Fly During the Years 1842 to 1846.* T. and W. Boone, 1847.

Kiki, Albert Maori, *Kiki, Ten Thousand Years in a Lifetime.* Pall Mall Press, 1968.

Lands of the Port Moresby-Kairuku Area, Papua New Guinea. Land Research Series No. 14, C.S.I.R.O., Australia, 1965.

Lawson, Captain J. A., *Wandering in the Interior of New Guinea.* Chapman and Hall, 1875.

Laurie, E. M. C., and Hill, J. E., *List of Land Mammals of New Guinea, Celebes and Adjacent Islands.* British Museum, 1954.

Levi, Herbert W., and Lorna R., *A Guide to Spiders and their Kin.* Golden Press, 1968.

McCarthy, J. K., *New Guinea.* F. W. Cheshire, 1968.

McCarthy, J. K., *New Guinea Journeys.* Robert Hale and Co., 1971.

McCarthy, J. K., *Our Nearest Neighbour.* F. W. Cheshire, 1963.

McCarthy, J. K., *Patrol into Yesterday: My New Guinea Years.* F. W. Cheshire, 1963.

Meek, A. S., *A Naturalist in Cannibal Land.* T. Fisher Unwin, 1913.

Moresby, Captain John, *Discoveries and Surveys in New Guinea and the D'Entrecasteaux Islands.* John Murray, 1876.

Murray, J. H. P., *Papua or British New Guinea.* T. Fisher Unwin, 1912.

Schmidt, Karl P., and Inger, Robert F., *Living Reptiles of the World.* Doubleday and Co., 1972.

Sinclair, J. P., *Behind the Ranges.* Melbourne University Press, 1966.

Souter, Gavin, *New Guinea: The Last Unknown.* Angus and Robertson, 1964.

Stuart, Ian, *Port Moresby.* Pacific Publications, 1970.

Rand, A. L., and Gilliard, E. T., *Handbook of New Guinea Birds.* Weidenfeld and Nicolson, 1967.

Ryan, John, *The Hot Land, Focus on New Guinea.* Macmillan and Co. Ltd., 1969.

Williams, R. M., *Stone Age Island.* Collins, 1964.

Acknowledgements

The author and editors of this book wish to thank the following: Tom Browne, London; Robin Cooke, Rabaul; Christopher Cooper, London; Tony and Jenny Crawford, National Cultural Council, Port Moresby; Dr. Philip Cribb, Royal Botanical Gardens, Kew; Charles Dettmer, Thames Ditton, Surrey; Max Downes, Department of Agriculture, Port Moresby; Lieutenant Commander B. Doxat-Pratt, Oxford; Julian C. Dring, British Museum (Natural History), London; John Gilbert, London; Miss A. G. C. Grandison, British Museum (Natural History), London; Richard Hills, London; Richard Humble, London; Norman H. Kolpas, London; Martin Leighton, London; Tony Long, Amsterdam; Mrs. Margaret Mackay, Port Moresby; C. McCarthy, British Museum (Natural History), London; Tony Matthews, Papua New Guinea Recruitment Office, London; Dr. Menzies, University of Papua New Guinea, Port Moresby; Mrs. Andrée Millar, University of Papua New Guinea, Port Moresby; Russell Miller, London; Geoffrey Palmer, East Grinstead, Sussex; Fred Parker, Department of Agriculture, Port Moresby; Roger Perry, Bradfield St. George, Suffolk; Professor P. W. Richards, University College of North Wales, Bangor; G. Strehler, Department of Forests, Boroko; R. T. Thompson, British Museum (Natural History), London; F. R. Wanless, British Museum (Natural History), London; Kevin White, Department of Forests, Port Moresby; Richard Zweifel, American Museum of Natural History, New York; The Zoological Society of London.

Index

*Numerals in italics indicate a
photograph or drawing of the subject
mentioned.*

Colour reproduction by P.D.I. Ltd., Leeds, England—a Time Inc. subsidiary.
Filmsetting by C. E. Dawkins (Typesetters) Ltd., London, SE1 1UN.
Printed and bound in Belgium by Brepols S.A.—Turnhout.